FIVE PILLARS
of a
TREMENDOUS
LIFE

FIVE PILLARS
of a
TREMENDOUS
LIFE

Inside Out Living
and
What Matters Most

David F. Pierce

TREMENDOUS
LIFE BOOKS.com

Five Pillars of a Tremendous Life

Published by
Tremendous Life Books
206 West Allen Street
Mechanicsburg, PA 17055

ISBN: 978-1-933715-84-1

Printed in the United States of America

Dedicated to

"Tremendous Howard"
and
"Tremendous Charlie"

Two great men who
discovered and followed their purpose in life,
defined leadership,
encouraged others continuously,
were giants in the faith,
and
loved others deeply, truly,
and tremendously.

Contents

Foreword

David Pierce has lived a tremendous life. Not because of his accomplishments or possessions, but because of the caliber of people he has surrounded himself with. He recognized their importance not only as family members, friends, or acquaintances, but as life-long mentors.

I met David and his lovely wife Debbie while on a business trip to Singapore in 2004. Dad had heard I was going overseas and immediately phoned David so that we could meet. During the meeting, it became apparent from the start that David and I both had fathers who bestowed many tremendous life lessons that enabled us to live our lives to the fullest.

Dad always told me that when the time came for his earthly departure, he wanted to go "home" on stage, microphone in hand, proclaiming his love of books and Christ. So it was not surprising that, at eighty years of age and ten years into his battle with cancer, he boarded a plane with his wife, Gloria, for a three-week overseas trip.

In fact, Christ was Dad's driving purpose—so much so that, during this last journey, it drove a public speaker who had lost his voice to take the stage half-way around the world in New Zealand, an event which served as the springboard for the *Five Pillars of a Tremendous Life* book and the documentary film, *A Tremendous Life: The Story of Charlie "Tremendous" Jones.*

It was that avid drive that inspired David to capture the essence of a tremendous life that forms the core of this book. Weeks after his return to the States, Dad's physical condition worsened and he was confined to hospice care. I got the chance to fly home every weekend to be with him. As we worked through the various programs and projects that were to continue long after his earthly departure, we were contacted by an amazing woman who had attended one of Dad's events during his recent overseas trip.

Qiujing, or "Q", as I came to know her, is a brilliant producer from New Zealand. Although she did not see him in his proverbial "hey day", she was so impressed with his message that she initiated the idea for a documentary film on his life. This would be done in conjunction with David Pierce, who hosted Dad's last seminar.

Dad was adamant that he not be the focus of this, but rather use it as an instrument to continue sharing the books, faith, and wisdom essential to living a tremendous life. And what better mouthpiece than David Pierce, who had shared so much of Dad's life paths, and the people who were so dear to Dad in his life.

Pillars are designed to be functional and strong. They serve as fundamental principles or practices that are prominent and may stand alone. I am thrilled that David has chosen to share these pillars with you because these pillars are meant to be shared. In fact, the book details the individuals who taught and inspired David to incorporate them into his life. And Q's film documented comments from many people close to Dad on the impact of the pillars in their own lives.

This was one of the last projects that Dad and I worked on together and I promised him I would see it to fruition. That would not have been possible without the talents and vision of David and Q, who worked countless hours creating, editing and reworking both products; Greg Dixon who worked to ensure the print layout and cover designs were perfect; Jason Liller, our Vice President of Operations, who contributed his editing skills to the manuscript as well, and the countless brothers and sisters in Christ who took the time out of their schedules to honor Dad at his Homegoing and contribute to the documentary.

Although the book and the documentary each stand alone, it is our hope that you would take advantage of utilizing both of them to reflect on the tremendous people and learning in your life. The Five Pillars aren't about changing the circumstances in your life. They are about how to best support your existing framework with five simple principles so *your* life can be tremendous too!

I'm sure Dad would have been pleased with the book and the documentary, and I hope you are too. Thank you Q. The documentary is tremendous. Thank you David for sharing the Five Pillars. And thank you dear reader for helping us change the world one book at a time.

Tracey C. Jones
President,
Tremendous Life Books
www.TremendousLifeBooks.com

Introduction

A s you read this book, you'll come across the word "tremendous" several hundred times. Tremendous is used over a dozen times in this Introduction alone...

Indeed I've had a tremendous life personally and professionally. And I've had a bountiful supply of tremendous people and experiences come my way ...as the Psalmist said my cup runneth over!

One of the greatest people in my life was even called "Tremendous"—Charles "Tremendous" Jones. He died about a year ago and is now a resident of Heaven.

The 100 million people who met Charlie and heard him speak or read his books would smile broadly to think of him crossing paths with Saint Peter. I can just see the scene...

Charlie holding Peter at arm's length with his hands tightly gripping Peter's shoulders and loudly asking "Peter? Not THE Peter?"...then hugging him tightly and kissing him on the cheek!

That was Charlie; author and teacher and speaker extraordinaire...a world renowned lover of books and reading. And as much as he promoted the virtues of reading and books, he said he never wanted a biography written about his life.

He always said there were better stories to read. I respectfully disagreed with him and still do but I'll honor his wish.While you'll read a lot about Charlie in this book, it is not a biography. It's not who Charlie was that's so important...it's what he did.

This is a book about the five pillars of a tremendous life...Charlie's life, and some others. It's also about what these five pillars mean to me and the role they've played in my life. But this isn't a book about my life either...

This book was written for you ... and about how the pillars can be applied to your life to help make it tremendous. You'll read about my mentors and heroes; those who taught me lessons in one or two or three of the pillars.

Then there are the three couples/people in my life who taught me about all five pillars; my dad and mom, Tremendous Howard and Tremendous Barbara, and of course Tremendous Charlie.

Tremendous Howard introduced me to Tremendous Charlie when I was just twelve years old. When I think about that introduction...that very moment in my life, I know now how blessed and fortunate I was to be standing in the company of these two great men. I miss them both so much and I think about them almost every day.

When I need to make a major decision or come across an unusual situation where I sure could benefit from wise counsel, I consult them...quietly...with my eyes closed. In a matter of seconds I can "see" them and "hear" them and I receive their advice...it's tremendous!

They taught me so much. I'm indebted to them forever. I loved these two men and they loved me. This book is dedicated to my loving memories of them both.

My Story and Life's Keychain

"Go confidently in the direction of your dreams...live the life you've imagined."
Henry David Thoreau

I've had a tremendous life...not because it's been easy. It hasn't. I've had my share of adversity, disappointment, disillusionment, heartbreak and heartache like most of us have.

...and not because I had money or my relatives did or some great benefactor did. They didn't. Money doesn't make for a tremendous life anyway even though some people sure do act and think like it does.

...not because I had a wealth of material and valuable things given to me. I didn't. Those things aren't necessary for a tremendous life either.

...and not because I won more than I lost or because I've been more positive than negative. I've lost many times. And as much as I don't like to admit it, I've been very negative and even cynical at times.

I used to think I had darker days and more troubles than most people; until others told me about their problems. Then I remembered my Tremendous "Grandma G" saying, "if we hung our troubles out on a line, you'd keep yours and I'd keep mine". She was right.

I also remember hearing Charlie "Tremendous" Jones tell an audience that they should never tell other people about personal problems. He said ten percent wouldn't care and the other ninety percent would be delighted! The audience laughed but they got the point. They knew he was right.

So why can I say in all honesty that I've had a tremendous life? Because I'm rich. Rich beyond my wildest dreams. Not the false and empty kind of rich as the world defines it...

My life has not been about how to "get rich" with money and wealth; it's been about how to "be rich" and enjoy the kind of richness that comes from inner peace and contentment. And it's been about recognizing what matters most.

Here's my story in relatively short form...

I was born in 1951 in Michigan, the youngest of four children. My parents loved each other deeply...every day of their 67 years together. Their love story was far better than anything any Hollywood writer could ever create.

Tremendous Carol, John, and Andy, my sister and brothers, remain among the greatest blessings of my life. While the four of us and our families are scattered from Asia Pacific to North Carolina and in between and we seldom see each other, we stay in close contact. My siblings are dear friends and trusted confidants and we love each other a lot.

Attending church was an important part of my life from my early days. I am a follower of Christ and my faith in God has been and will always matter most to who I am, what I do, and why I do it.

I went to public schools. I believe Midwestern public schools were among the best in the 1950s and 1960s. According to the U.S. Department of Education, they still are. The lessons I learned about life in school were wonderful. My teachers, classmates, coaches and principals were tremendous.

Going to school with a mix of kids from a wide range of ethnic backgrounds, family income brackets, differing faiths and political stripes helped make me more well-rounded than the kids in my neighborhood who attended private schools with little diversity in student population or in opinions and thoughts.

Playing team sports was a big part of my life from age eight to age 23. My experiences and lessons in little league football and school teams in football, basketball, and track & field were all tremendous. I went on to play football in college, which paid for most of my undergraduate education.

I was fortunate enough to sign a contract with the Washington Redskins in the National Football League. I didn't make the team but it was a tremendous experience to try out in the big leagues.

After football, I started my adult working life with jobs in management. Five years later, I found a career opportunity and jumped in with both feet. I've never looked back. It has been more rewarding than I ever could have imagined.

I celebrated my 30th Anniversary in the life insurance industry this year. What a tremendous career it has been. I've worked my way through the ranks from Agent to CEO. During my career, I've worked in fifteen different countries and lived in the United States, Singapore, Hong Kong, and New Zealand. There will likely be a few more ports of call before I retire and I look forward to them.

I often tell people that I'm not in the insurance business, but rather that *it* is in *me*. I've witnessed first-hand the miracle of what life and health insurance has done in the lives of customers. The insurance industry has brought purpose to my life and given me a chance to serve others in countless tremendous ways.

It's been a joy to help bring others into the business and to help them grow and become successful. And it's been very rewarding to play a role in helping life and health insurance companies grow and prosper.

During my career, I worked hard to continue my education, completing two master's degrees and three life insurance industry professional designations. I agree with Benjamin Franklin's advice that "your education shouldn't stop until you do". The things I learned and have been able to apply have been tremendous.

I was asked to join the Adjunct Faculty of Western Kentucky University in the late 1980s as a part-time Professor of

Communication. I said yes and I loved teaching.

When I moved to Tennessee in the mid-1990s, I was asked to join the Adjunct Faculty of Middle Tennessee State University and teach Life and Health Insurance courses in the Economics and Business School. I agreed and loved teaching insurance studies as much as I loved teaching communication.

What tremendous experiences I had teaching and what great memories I have from those days.

Adult family life has been a big part of why my life has been tremendous. My experiences with marriage, two tremendous children, and four wonderful grandchildren are big parts of my story. I've known firsthand about the happiness and fulfillment of a good marriage… and unfortunately, the pain when a marriage fails and ends.

I've been in a great marriage for twelve years…and it just keeps getting better. My wonderful wife, Tremendous Debbie, left her career to follow me around the world. While it may sound exotic and glamorous to say you've lived in this or that foreign country, the truth is it's very difficult and quite lonely adjusting to different cultures…and being so far away from family and friends.

Debbie has risen to the occasion and is my rock. I love her so much and I'm so happy she's in my life. What a lucky guy I am!

I've known about the joys and challenges of parenting and becoming a grandparent. I've also known what it's like to live on the other side of the world and see my children and grandchildren only rarely and briefly. It's tough…very tough.

Then there's my avocation; singing. From junior high school and high school choruses to church choirs to professional choruses, singing has provided a tremendous break from my "regular life". I cannot find the words to adequately express what gifts I've received from music and what music has meant to me.

I've sung professionally in Orchestra Hall in Minneapolis with The Minnesota Bach Society, in Severance Hall in Cleveland and Carnegie Hall in New York with The Cleveland Orchestra

Chorus, and in The Esplanade in Singapore with The Singapore Symphony Orchestra Chorus.

These accomplishments in education, sports, family, music, and business have not, unto themselves, made my life tremendous. But they've contributed mightily to it.

I've focused on the high points of my story, the successes and accomplishments. The low points were temporary setbacks and distractions and opportunities to learn, to pick myself up and to try again or start over.

Like you, I've been a lot of places, done a lot of things and met a lot of people. My life is unique and special to me. Your life is just as unique and just as special to you, and it should be.

I encourage you to think back through your life and make a list of your accomplishments. You might just be surprised to discover how tremendous your life has been. And the good news is that there's more of life to go! Thank God for that.

Socrates said an unexamined life isn't worth living. I agree. Take stock and examine your life. How's the "education of you" going?

The experiences along the way with people, events and ideas in my life have been a course of study I like to call "Life 101". Then there's something called "The College of Hard Knocks", learning life's tough lessons when things go wrong. I've attended that school too.

We all have. My mom has always reminded me that "we grow on the bumps" as we go down the road of life, not the smooth parts.

The bumps along my journey have been numerous. They've included divorce, finances going up then going down then going up and down again, a long list of physical challenges and surgeries from years of knock 'em, sock 'em, rough and tumble sports, and of course there have been a lot of disappointments and failures along the way.

Despite the downturns and the setbacks, my life has indeed been tremendous. Here's why…

It's not what happened to me in life and whether it was good or bad that made my life tremendous…it was how I dealt with success and failure. It's how I accepted the accolades as well as the adversity, what lessons I learned and how I applied them when the next bump in the road came my way.

Charles Swindoll said, "life is 10% what happens to you and 90% how you deal with it". He was talking about attitude… and he was 100% correct.

For me, making life tremendous meant I could apply the lessons learned about values and personal virtues from my dad and mom and find real contentment.

The well-known maxim says "children learn what they live". How true. Thanks to my dad and mom, I lived and learned a lot of tremendous things.

I was taught to respect others, at school, in my neighborhood and at church. This respect was color blind, it knew no social status and it had no litmus test of someone's politics or personal beliefs.

I was taught to tell the truth; to admit when I was wrong and ask for forgiveness…to genuinely use the words "please" and "thank you" and "you're welcome" and "I'm sorry".

My dad taught me well that if I couldn't manage my time, I wouldn't be able to manage anything else, and to this day I show up on time, end on time, and manage my time.

I was taught the benefits of having integrity and discipline and being accountable and responsible and trustworthy…to stand on my own two feet and be independent…to be confident enough to be myself yet humble enough to know my limits…to not feel sorry for myself… and to laugh at myself in a healthy way…

I was taught that my word should be my bond…to finish what I started and to clean up my own messes.

I was taught to honor and obey my parents…and how to show genuine love and caring for my brothers and sister.

I learned that faith in God and study and prayer made sense

of life and helped me find order and understanding to both God's plan and the effects of human free will.

I was taught to be genuinely grateful and how to give thanks...why and how to praise others...to play fair and play hard...to win graciously and lose graciously...that cheaters never win and winners never cheat.

I learned how to get back up and dust myself off after getting knocked down, or let down or lied to, or treated unfairly...and that failure in a project does not constitute failure in life.

I was taught to read and to ask questions.

I was taught about the vagaries of the human condition... that aging and death are a part of the natural order of things... and should be accepted with grace and gratitude.

My parents spent quality time with me and they encouraged me in whatever course of study I wanted to pursue, whatever sport I wanted to play, whatever musical instrument I wanted to play, whatever project I wanted to do.

They listened to me. They were genuinely interested in me and in my life and in my personal and spiritual growth. They equipped me for life and for living it to the fullest.

Their teaching tools included the Bible, World Book Encyclopedia, the best set they could find of classical music recordings, and a long list of magazines and periodicals that were wholesome. Wholesome...but David, you may say, isn't that an old-fashioned word? Who wants to be wholesome? We did back then. I still do.

Indeed, my dad and mom gave me so much...strong personal, family, spiritual, and societal values. Tremendous things that serve me well and always have.

The greatest gift my parents gave me was confidence. They knew that decision making was one of the most important things in life. They equipped me with the ability and confidence to make decisions. They also taught me to live with the decisions I made.

I was given a lot of keys for "life's keychain" as was once explained to me. Dad and mom gave me a lot of keys, as did the other heroes and giants in my life.

Life's keychain is an analogy about life and learning and living life to the fullest. I love it. Here's how it goes…

As we have a new learning experience in life we're "given" a key. This is the key of understanding. If we're smart we don't misplace the key. Instead we put it on our keychain. Our keychain grows as we live and it gets larger and larger as we learn more and get more keys.

When and as we encounter circumstances in life that require decisions, we pull out our keychain and know exactly where the right key can be found. We use it to unlock the best solution…to make the best decision.

The person who first told me about this analogy was Tremendous Jimmy. He was eighteen years older than me, was my business partner for a decade, and one of my best friends in life. I often marveled at how quickly he could find keys and knew what to do. He used to tell me he was "just a little bit farther down life's path and that he had a larger keychain".

He let me know what was likely ahead of me on life's path. A few weeks before Jimmy died, he told me he had given me all of his keys I needed and that the balance of my life would be tremendous. He was right.

The biggest and most well-worn keys on my keychain are the lessons taught to me by Tremendous Howard and Tremendous Barbara, by Tremendous Mal, my college football coach; by Tremendous Doug, my high school choral director and music teacher; by Tremendous Jimmy; and of course by Charlie "Tremendous" Jones, my mentor and friend.

Charlie had his own version of Life's Keychain. He said it was God who gave us all the empty keychain at birth. You can read his version in Appendix B…see law Number Five of his *7 Laws of Leadership*.

How about you and your life? How about your teachers,

your mentors, your coaches, your role models? What have you learned from them? What keys did they give you? Do you use them? And do you help others by giving them a key for their keychain?

You'll see more references to life's keychain in this book. It's a great way to think about gaining experience and learning lessons in life...then applying what you've learned...recognizing what matters most, and realizing that life can indeed be tremendous.

"We succeed in enterprises which demand the positive qualities we possess, but we excel in those which can also make use of our defects."
Alexis de Tocqueville

Charlie "Tremendous" Jones
and the Five Pillars

"Know-how is tremendous when you know-why;
know-how lets you drive it, knowing-why drives you."
Charles "Tremendous" Jones

From 1963 to 2008, in one way or another, Charlie Jones came into my life. I first heard him speak in 1963 when my Dad hired him as a fledgling new face on the public speaking circuit.

I was just twelve years old the first time I heard Charlie speak. He was speaking at a Men's Retreat at a Christian camp and conference in Michigan where Tremendous Howard served faithfully as Executive Director for 25 years.

Dad introduced me to Charlie. Charlie patted me on the head and said "David my young man, life is tremendous!"…and he said it loudly.

Charlie was a very, very funny man. What a sense of humor he had and how well he employed it to tell his stories and make his points. The men were rolling in the aisles. But he was also imparting deep truths about his *7 Laws of Leadership* and about doing the right thing.

He talked enthusiastically about personal and family values and about being an encourager of others, about sharing faith, about love and about finding purpose in life.

It was that day that I first heard him say something I would hear him say over and over again during the next 45 years:

"You are the same today as you'll be in five years, except for two things; the people you meet and the books you read."

He was tremendous. And he became well-known the world over during the next four decades. He was ranked in the Top Twenty Speakers of the Last Century and he inspired and influenced over 100 million people.

I saw and heard Charlie over the decades at conferences, seminars, sales rallies, success symposiums, life insurance industry sales congresses and road-shows. I read what he wrote. I developed a lasting personal friendship with him…often calling him during the last seven years from whatever foreign country I called home.

I'll never forget calling him from Asia or the South Pacific. He'd answer…I'd say, "Charlie…it's David"…then he'd say "Not THE Tremendous David?" What tremendous memories! In fact, the telephone played a major role in my relationship with Charlie…

After calling my dad and mom to tell them I had entered the life insurance business in 1980, Charlie was the next call. He was so happy for me and so proud.

He encouraged me in my personal life, my professional life and my spiritual life. And because he too was, as he put it, "an insurance man", we shared a lot of life's deeper truths about selling and service during long phone conversations over the years.

I cherish the nickname Charlie had for me. He called me "Beloved". He of course knew that David means "beloved" in Hebrew and that in the Bible, David "was a man after God's own heart". He had a certain way to pronounce it when he called me Beloved, a certain lilt and warmth in his voice, filled with love.

He was one of the biggest encouragers in my life. The biggest compliment I ever received came from Charlie; he once told me in an e-mail that I was "one in a billion". Quite a thing to hear from the guy I consider one in a trillion!

And of course he always sent me books. Lots of books.

Charlie's love of books developed from reading them by the

hundreds...several hundreds. He became an author and an excellent one at that...his *Life Is Tremendous* has sold into the millions.

He encouraged others to read. His favorite speech about reading ended with:

> "Don't read to be smart, read to be real.
> Don't read to be big, read to be down to earth.
> Don't read to memorize, read to realize.
> Don't read to learn, read to unlearn a lot of things you never should have learned in the first place.
> And don't read a lot, read just enough to get your mind stimulated and thinking and get you curious and hungry to keep you learning all your life!"

In 2001, when my dad was terminally ill with cancer, I called Charlie and asked him if he'd give dad a call. He enthusiastically said yes. Mom reported to me a few days later that Charlie and Tremendous Howard talked and prayed and laughed for close to an hour. She said it was tremendous.

Charlie and Tremendous Gloria's daughter Tracey were coming to Singapore on business a few years ago when Debbie and I lived there. Charlie called me and asked if we would please meet up with her. We did; it was tremendous to meet Tracey and talk about my experiences with her dad over the decades.

Tracey loved my imitation of Charlie. So have a few others over the years, especially Tremendous Lindsay and Lynne, dear friends and business colleagues in New Zealand. Lindsay once told Charlie, "David does a better you than *you* do!"

If imitation is the sincerest form of flattery then I flatter Charlie a lot. I can't help it. When I speak publicly or with my mom or siblings or Tremendous Tracey or Lindsay and Lynne; and when I start to really drive home my point, out comes my version of Charlie T. Jones. It's his intonation, word choices, gestures, enthusiasm, and passion!

I told you earlier that laughter was Charlie's best tool. He used laughter to get people to laugh at themselves and at life. Just when his audiences would be laughing the most, Charlie would drive home his point by imparting wisdom and insight and truth and winning ways to treat others and handle life.

In 2007 Charlie called me to inform me that at age eighty he was planning a "final world tour". I asked him why he said *final*…and he told me he had cancer, again. He had cancer a few years earlier which had miraculously disappeared…and now it was back. He said the prognosis was not good but he wasn't going to quit.

I told him he must come to New Zealand and I gave him my personal guarantee that we'd pack an auditorium to hear him speak. He agreed to come.

What an event it was…22 May 2008…one of the greatest days of my life.

Charlie's final world tour ended up being just one appearance…the New Zealand event. Tremendous Charlie was "tremendously terminally ill" I told the audience. The disease had taken his vision in one eye. He was weak and had to lean on the podium. Worse yet for a speaker, the cancer had claimed his voice.

So this giant of a man who had helped over 100 million people, this holder of countless keys on his keychain did what a true professional would be expected to do…

He didn't quit. He whispered. The audience ate up every word, every joke, every truth he shared. It was a grand final appearance in Charlie's tremendous career. He died a few months later at his home in Pennsylvania.

I'm so blessed and so fortunate to have had this great person in my life. To think that my dad helped him get his speaking career started is something that's very special to me. To have Charlie tell me "oh my Beloved, I'm so glad I got to end my career with you"…well, there are no words to tell you what that means to me. I get a big lump in my throat just thinking about it.

We videotaped the event in New Zealand. The filmmaker, Qiujing ("Q" for short) was so taken with Charlie and his message that she and Dean, a great guy to whom she is engaged, envisioned making a documentary film about his life.

I called Charlie to see if he was interested in this documentary idea. He loved it. Knowing he was near death, he saw the project as a tremendous way to continue getting his message out to others and he fully endorsed it.

Tremendous Q and I began a long series of e-mails with Tremendous Tracey about the work to be done. She promised to shepherd the project. The documentary was filmed and the process of editing and development was about to begin when Q and Tracey asked me to continue being involved in telling Charlie's story.

They were focusing on his main themes and messages and the keys he gave to millions for their keychains. They asked me what all of that meant to me personally. They asked for my opinion and input on the documentary. Then they asked me for something else that I wasn't expecting…

They were convinced the best way to release the documentary was to have a book "simultaneously released" with it as part of a package. I told Q that I thought that was a great idea. Then Q informed me she and Tracey thought that I should be the one to write the book!

They wanted me to write the book from my experience and my perspectives about what Tremendous Charlie and Tremendous Howard and other mentor-heroes had done for me. They wanted me to tell my story and how my life was influenced by these great people.

I was honored to be asked and felt compelled to say "yes".

Like many people, I've had thoughts about maybe writing a book "someday". And now I'd agreed to write a book in my spare time while leading a life insurance company plus all the other commitments of family and life.

Five Pillars of a Tremendous Life

Did I say spare time? Who has spare time? No matter. I accepted the challenge and after all, I was getting to write about Charlie and my dad and mom and others. The book was a labor of love and as I began to organize what I might say and how I'd say it, my hope was that the book would offer readers something of value.

I thoroughly enjoyed the writing and editing, no matter how early in the morning or late in the evening or on weekends and holidays. My prayer is that this book will be useful and meaningful to you.

Charlie's messages were many. He talked a lot about commitment and not quitting. He used humor so well. He told his audiences to be encouragers and to create a positive environment.

He shared what God had done in his life and could do in theirs. And he talked about loving family and others through effective leadership and lots of good old-fashioned enthusiasm.

His messages overlapped and were woven together in a beautiful tapestry. No wonder he was recognized as one of the greatest speakers of the last 100 years.

No surprise he touched the hearts and minds of over 100 million people. What a man...and what a legacy! (See Appendix A to get a full dose of Charlie "Tremendous" Jones)

My challenge was to talk about Charlie AND others...and to make it MY story, not Charlie's. So I set out to find the best way to write this book...

Charlie's life indeed was a tremendous life. So were the lives of my mentors. Was there a common theme to what they gave me...to the keys I now owned that reflected their influence? I determined there was.

My heroes provided training, guidance and support in one or more of five disciplines of life that I think of as pillars. I chose the term "pillars" because it indicates the disciplines are foundational, supporting, visible, separate, yet reliant on each other and they stand firm over time.

The five pillars are **Purpose**, **Leadership**, **Encouragement**, **Faith** …and **Love**.

To me, the pillars are circular, not linear. They form the foundation not only for my tremendous life, and my mentor's tremendous lives, I believe they can be the foundation for *your* tremendous life.

The pillars can work for you no matter what color your skin is or what your ethnic background is or what language you speak or what your chosen faith is.

It doesn't matter what your age or marital status is, where you live, what you do for a living, or where you are on any social or economic register.

The pillars are central to my life. And I've seen them produce tremendous results for the people who've meant so much to me throughout my life.

Mal and Doug, my football coach and my music teacher, taught me unforgettable life lessons in leadership and encouragement. Jimmy, my business partner and best friend, honed my skills in purpose and love. As I wrote several pages back, Tremendous Charlie, my dad and my mom mentored me in all five pillars.

Knowing how to maximize the lessons I've been learning in the five pillars are some of the most used keys on my keychain. Writing this book is my way to give you these keys.

Don't worry about the bumps in the road ahead. Be courageous and be bold. Use your keys with confidence.

You already have more keys than you think you have. I encourage you to use them…and to unlock the doors to a tremendous life.

"Courage is nothing less than the power to overcome danger…misfortune…fear…injustice…
while continuing to affirm inwardly that life…
with all its sorrows…is good…

Five Pillars of a Tremendous Life

that everything is meaningful
even if in a sense beyond our understanding...
and that there is always tomorrow."
Dorothy Thompson

Inside Out Living

"What lies before us and what lies behind us are small matters compared to what lies within us, and when we bring what is within us out into the world, miracles happen."
Ralph Waldo Emerson

Before we examine the pillars, I need to clear the air. This book isn't about you having a wonderful life that is centered on yourself. I think it's important to put the pillars into he proper context and perspective.

Sharing a true story about what happened to me recently describes what I mean…

While on my annual home leave to the United States in 2008, I visited several bookstores and discovered that I couldn't find the "Self Help" section.

I couldn't find this section in the bookstores I visited, and thought surely it hadn't disappeared. A helpful clerk in one store assured me that it was still there but the name had changed: it was called "Personal Development" at one store and "Personal Growth" at another.

There's good and bad news about these newly titled sections…

The good news is that if you search long enough, you'll be able to find some truly "self help" books. The bad news is that the vast majority of the new books and titles are overwhelmingly about one topic: YOU.

I saw books about:
        you getting rich…or richer
        you becoming thin

you owning more things
you impressing others
you getting more things in life
you looking better
you looking younger
you living longer, and
well … you get my point.

Are we that self-centered and selfish…is this what matters most to us? Lord, I hope not!

The new "personal growth" sections signal a shift in focus away from the old goal of improving our inner-selves so we can help make others and the world better to a new focus that seems to be based on conspicuous consumption, self-absorption, and by an approach to life that says "it's all about me".

As I walked out of bookstore after bookstore I concluded a lot of people have apparently misplaced, forgotten, lost, or forsaken important values about what's important in life and what can make life tremendous.

What makes life tremendous is not about you, it's about what you can do for others.

Taking advice from the outside and developing it internally, keeping it internally and just for ourselves is what I call "Outside In Living". And if there's little or no "pay it forward" and no sharing and no "others" in the mix, then I don't think life can ever become tremendous.

What makes life tremendous is taking in life's lessons and the keys we're given then directing ourselves and our efforts outwardly to help others. That's "Inside Out Living" and that indeed is tremendous.

The first time I heard Zig Ziglar speak was at a Positive Thinking Rally in Minneapolis in 1978. How well I remember him saying "you'll get enough of what you want out of life if you help enough other people get what they want out of life". He was absolutely right. That's Inside Out Living at it's best.

Something else I heard Zig Ziglar and Art Linkletter and other motivational speakers say on many occasions is "people don't care how much you know until they know how much you care". That's Inside out Living...no doubt about it.

An Inside out life is "switched-on" and pointed in the right direction. When the focus is what you can do for others, good things happen for them...and for you.

It may sound a bit corny to you, but I remember a poster on display at our church when I was a young boy. From a distance all you could read was the word JOY, but when you got closer you could see additional details. The "J" was for Jesus...the "O" was for others...and the "Y" was for you. That was clearly the order of things, and the result was joy in life. Corny? Not to me.

When I look back at the influence my heroes had on my life, it was understanding their purpose, benefiting from their leadership, receiving their encouragement, seeing their faith, and receiving their love that made them heroes and giants to me. They paid it forward. They lived life inside out.

It was their acts of giving and their willingness to give that made what they did and said so valuable and so positive. Giving is a common thread running through all five pillars.

Life is not about "getting" nor, as some think, "giving to get". Tremendous Charlie always reminded audiences that giving to get was not giving but rather was actually "trading". He said it was all about giving. Giving, whether you get or not...giving. Giving to give...giving for the sheer pleasure of giving.

This concept about giving was important to Charlie...see Number Three of Charlie's *7 Laws of Leadership* in Appendix B.

Back to my bookstore experience...

Some may say the whole shift from "self-help" to "personal growth or development" is nothing more than semantics. I disagree. Check it out for yourself. Go down to your local bookstore and have a look. Be ready to be disappointed; you'll have to search hard to find books on values or faith or purpose…or helping others.

The bookstore experience reminded me of something else; humorous on one hand but on the other hand very profound …

Sometime in the 1980s I watched a stand-up comedian on a late night TV show perform a comedy routine about magazines and how they related to life. He talked about being a kid in the 1950s and 1960s when the magazines in his home had titles and perspectives as "big", he said with outstretched arms, as LOOK and LIFE and TIME.

Then in the 1970s a new magazine came out. It was called "just" PEOPLE he said, bringing his open hands within inches of each other. Then in the last year or so another new magazine came out called "simply" US he said, with the thumb and forefinger of one hand almost touching.

He predicted it would only be a matter of time before we'd see a new magazine called "only" ME he said, as he pointed to his chest with emphasis. The audience loved it and laughed a lot. How prophetic this comedian was.

I think if he performed that routine today, he'd likely add another title: NOW he would say as he might slap his hands together.

In addition to a lot of people becoming extremely selfish, it seems there's a need for instant gratification. No waiting or saving or earning or building up; but getting and having the best or the latest of everything…right now.

This is not an indictment on everyone. I know we're not all so selfish, and thank God for that!

There are a lot of great people who agree with Woodrow Wilson that there is "a higher form of human life… community". There are millions who have given of themselves and their money and their time and their talents in service to help others.

The lessons learned from my heroes are that the pillars of a tremendous life are "about" just that…they're about making a positive difference in the lives of others.

They're about giving and helping others find their purpose in life, helping others develop leadership skills for life, encouraging others to move forward and upward in life, sharing faith and doing positive things in other's lives through faith, and openly and genuinely loving others.

This is the perspective and context I wanted to make clear regarding the five pillars of a tremendous life. As you go through the following chapters, I encourage you to apply what I've written about the pillars to your personal and professional lives.

Have you discovered purpose in your life? Is life tremendous for you? If so, that's good news. If not, you can start today to live your life with a focus on what matters most in life.

Examine your life. Be honest with yourself. Start leading your life. Take charge of your time and your attitude and your outlook.

Start encouraging others to reach meaningful goals. Encourage them to stay the course and not give in, give up or quit. Encourage them to finish that class or to read that book or to work for that promotion. By encouraging them you will be encouraged and uplifted.

Weave your faith into everything you do and say. The more you do it, the more confident you'll become. You'll discover that it's okay to stand up and be counted for your faith, especially if it's genuine and compassionate and real.

Give yourself permission to love others like never before; when you do, you'll become more lovable. You'll be able to teach others that the really bad four-letter words are hate and fear; and that they can be overcome and conquered by the best four-letter word of all...love.

And you'll learn more about another tremendous four-letter word: hope. Hope is a wonderful thing and is present in every one of the five pillars.

With hope much can be accomplished. Without it life becomes mere existence. I believe a tremendous life is filled with hope...and purpose...and leadership....and encouragement…and faith…and love.

It's your life. Be a leader. Choose happiness. See the best in every person, every day and in every situation, especially in tough situations where things aren't going as you'd planned.

Make life tremendous no matter what your station in life; no matter how much education or money or friends or success you have or don't have.

And while you're at it, make your family tremendous, make your workplace tremendous, make your house of worship tremendous, make your school or local organization or club tremendous.

I believe you can touch every life that comes your way every day and help make their lives better. That's Inside Out Living…and …it's tremendous!

"Only those who dare to fail greatly
can ever achieve greatly."
John F. Kennedy

The Pillar of Purpose

"The purpose of life is not to be happy. It is to be useful, to be honorable, to be compassionate, to have it make some difference that you have lived, and lived well."
Ralph Waldo Emerson

Discovering and developing purpose in life provides answers to questions like why you're here and what you're supposed to be doing with your life. Having purpose in your life helps make it tremendous. It's about Inside Out Living and giving and others.

A great example from classical literature of someone discovering purpose in their life is crusty old Ebenezer Scrooge in *A Christmas Carol,* by Charles Dickens. As you read the story, you meet a guy who lives life Outside In and is about as selfish as one can be. In time, he sees the error of his ways and what life, and death for that matter, could be like if he continues to live his life as he has.

You know the rest of the story. He does change his ways. He realizes life is much better when lived Inside Out. And along the way, he finds purpose and happiness for himself as he brings happiness to others.

Fyodor Dostoyevsky, said "the secret of man's being is not only to live but to have something to live for". What do you live for? What would you say is your purpose in life?

Some people can easily answer these questions. Maybe you can. Or maybe you haven't thought about it yet because you've been too busy completing your education or you're in the early stages of career and family life.

Five Pillars of a Tremendous Life

When you find purpose in your life, your focus is not you...nor is it about any kind of temporal or fleeting happiness. Helen Keller said "many persons have a wrong idea of what constitutes true happiness. It is not attained through self-gratification but through fidelity to a worthy purpose".

Your purpose may be your vocation. That may depend on whether you fell into your job or career as some do or you felt a calling and sensed a passion to do what you do. Some might say a "calling" is reserved for the ministry or missionary work. No way.

I've known people who felt called to a life of helping others in the medical field or in professional service industries such as financial services, accounting, and law.

And I've known policemen and policewomen, firefighters and teachers who believed they were called to do what they do because it provided deep and lasting fulfillment and purpose to their lives. I wouldn't discount any profession or job by saying it couldn't be part of a life of purpose.

I know a woman in Hong Kong who would proudly tell you that her purpose in life is to work long hours doing hard menial labor, as she has for many years, in order to put her four children through university and one through medical school. Not one bit of her work is glamorous but it's given her purpose and pride and contentment.

Purpose could come from an avocation or hobby. I knew an elderly fellow in Minnesota who worked on trains for a living and his retirement hobby was to build model trains and miniature train yards.

His passion involved going to elementary schools and teaching young students about how America was "built" on the rails. He said his purpose in life was "to preserve the legacy of the locomotive".

You might be asked to volunteer at school or church or at a social club or community center for what appears to be a small and relatively simple project or special event. You might agree to give of your time and talents and before you know it, you've discovered purpose in helping others.

It could happen. It has happened to millions of people. That's what service to others often does.

Purpose may be something you do with your hands or your time or your money or in sharing your life experience in teaching and counseling and mentoring others. Many people have found purpose in discovering new ways to serve others and do things for the greater good.

But whatever it is and whether it's one or two or more things that bring meaning and purpose to your life, you'd better be ready. Get your proverbial seat backs and tray tables in their upright and locked positions…because when you discover purpose in life, fulfilling that purpose can and often does consume a lot of your time and energy.

You won't complain a bit though because it will be a labor of love.

There's no doubt that purpose in life is a driving force. It's not just about vision and passion, it's also about action. The kind of action that gets things done for the cause and for the benefit of making others better, and making the world a better place.

Sometimes purpose is more like a relentless pursuit. Benjamin Disraeli wrote, "I have brought myself by long meditation to the conviction that a human being with a settled purpose must accomplish it, and that nothing can resist a will which will stake even existence upon its fulfillment".

People with purpose in life are some of the most positive and enthusiastic and caring people you'll ever know. And they never quit. Never.

They have tremendous persistence. No matter how tough the going gets they see it through. They get the job done because they see what they do as part of their mission in life.

It's because they care. It's because they are a part of something that is larger than themselves. It's because they are making a difference, a positive difference. And it shows in how they walk, how they talk, how they act, what they do, and how they treat others.

People with purpose exhibit what my dad and mom called a "servant heart". They have loads of extra energy. They're almost always "on their front foot" and are focused. They have a sweet and loving and accepting and positive attitude about what happens in life, good or bad.

Their outlook on life and their perspective about life is healthy and positive. They laugh easily. And they often cry easily too as they're moved by deep passion and conviction for others. And they believe in what they're doing and what the positive results will be. They're happy to serve others and know that service is tremendous!

Albert Schweitzer said, "the purpose of human life is to serve, and to show compassion and the will to help others".

Compassion is a common trait seen in a person who has found his or her purpose. Other common traits include strong ethical and moral values, integrity, living up to expectations, genuine and authentic respect and love of people, sensible life priorities, and emotional strength.

I trust you're beginning to see why I believe purpose is a pillar of a tremendous life.

How do you find purpose in your life? I think the answer lies in the specific circumstances of your life…and I think it's highly personal. But I'm quite sure you'll know when you've found purpose in life.

My experience says you'll know because you'll feel a sense of fulfillment and you'll know you're making a significant and meaningful difference in other's lives for all the right reasons. You'll have clarity and you'll sense contentment and satisfaction.

As I said earlier, it's likely you'll find several things and causes and opportunities to bring purpose to your life.

I found purpose in teaching and mentoring my children and now their children, albeit from great distances. And I've always sensed purpose in having serious talks with siblings and nieces and nephews about important life topics like history, education, faith, family, love, financial responsibilities, death and dying.

I found purpose in my life by taking a leadership position whether appointed or not to help business groups or teams or organizations reach their goals.

It's also been a purpose in my life to help others get more out of their careers by advancing to another company, or being able to secure a higher rank or position, or to get to a new location with their current employer, or to obtain more education, or to start their own business.

I also found purpose as a volunteer and fund-raiser, then a board member of an internationally recognized non-profit organization that works to eliminate premature birth and birth defects.

And it has always brought purpose to my life to live and share my faith Inside Out.

Tremendous Charlie had several purposes throughout his life; family, career, speaking, lover of books, publisher and more. His list was a very long one.

His life's main purpose was sharing his faith in hopes of bringing more people to a personal relationship with Jesus Christ. He also found purpose in teaching his *7 Laws of Leadership* and in exhorting others to "be an encourager". He saw purpose and value in loving others and in doing things for them that showed his love. Charlie found purpose in all five pillars.

Tremendous Howard found purpose in family and his work. He walked away from a promising corporate career in accounting when he felt called to the leadership of a Christian camp and conference. I could write another book, with mom's help of course, about the lives he touched and changed in over a quarter of a century through his calling.

My sister, Tremendous Carol, found purpose throughout her nursing career. After working in hospitals, doctor's offices, and nursing homes, she thoroughly enjoyed the last part of her career working in hospice care. No ordinary nurse was she! She went way beyond the call of duty...

She sang her patient's old favorite hymns to them and she developed close relationships with their families. She shared her Christian faith and lived out her values in how she attended to others and helped them maintain their dignity.

My brothers, Tremendous John and Tremendous Andy, served others through their careers and personal lives. John was a teacher and a coach. Andy was a cop. They moved on to careers in sales, management, and leadership. They've touched so many lives and made such a positive difference in the lives of so many people.

Andy and John also found purpose in helping their "little brother" in countless ways. I thank God every time I recall how they helped me, pushed me, taught me, supported me, encouraged me, and loved me unconditionally.

Tremendous Jimmy was a lawyer who taught at law schools as an Adjunct Faculty member as a part-time purpose. Then he founded a law school with some like-minded folks from scratch! Then he helped start one of the largest non-profit organizations focused on a health care issue in the U.S.

He also built a Trust Department from scratch in Minnesota's largest privately-owned bank. Jimmy always liked to share his "Maxims" about life with clients and friends and bank customers. You'll find his Maxims in Appendix C.

Tremendous Doug was passionate about the difference between singing notes and making music. He taught me that perfectionism builds walls and that we should never strive for perfection but instead do our very best. He was the very model of dedication to music and to his students.

He was tough on us and we loved him for it. He made us better young people. He'd encourage us to do better when we did not perform well and congratulate us when we did. These may seem like small things but they're not. They can have a huge impact…and Doug did on thousands of students.

Tremendous Mal was much, much more than a college football Coach; he shaped lives. His purpose was not so much focused on winning games as it was seeing young men get a university education and be equipped for life from the lessons learned in football.

He also showed his players that a tough guy on the field of play can be a tender and loving dad off the field as he was to his five daughters.

Coach Mal was the best coach I ever had…and I had a lot of coaches in football and other sports. His passion for excellence and his ability to encourage his players was incredible. He was an optimist and an encourager and a true leader in every sense.

I know you could write about your heroes as I have about mine. You'd share about the gifts you received from them; the keys they gave you for your keychain. You'd write with conviction about the role of purpose in their lives and what that meant to you and your life. There's no doubt purpose is a pillar of a tremendous life…as I'm sure your heroes have shown you.

What are you passionate about in terms of serving and helping others? What are your gifts and skills in terms of something you can do or something you can share that is fulfilling to you and benefits others?

Discover purpose in your life, or maybe I should say allow purpose to discover *you*, and let it use you to uplift others to better and more meaningful lives.

"This is the true joy in life, the being used for a purpose recognized by yourself as a mighty one; the being thoroughly worn out before you are thrown on the scrap heap; the being a force of nature instead of a feverish selfish little clod of ailments and grievances complaining that the world will not devote itself to making you happy."
George Bernard Shaw

The Pillar of Leadership

"Lives of great men all remind us
We can make our lives sublime,
And, departing, leave behind us
Footprints in the sands of time."
Henry Wadsworth Longfellow

Much has been said and written about leadership in the last fifteen to twenty years. It's clearly a hot topic that's getting hotter for good reason.

The world is desperately in need of true leadership at many levels; in families, in business, in government, in organizations, in schools, in places of worship, in communities, in nations, and in people's personal lives.

Why is leadership a pillar of a tremendous life? Because leadership is about being responsible and being accountable. It's about seizing opportunities to show the way to others. It's about improving yourself and others. It's about being a decision maker. It's about taking action.

Tremendous Charlie was decades ahead of his time on this topic. He developed and talked about his *7 Laws of Leadership* in the 1960s. His truths on leadership were not only applicable to being a leader of others; they were just as applicable to developing leadership in your own life. You'll find them in Appendix B.

It doesn't matter if you're an appointed or elected leader or not. Becoming a leader often involves something as simple as setting a positive example or being a good role model.

Leaders sometimes reach out to others in proactive ways to

44

help them or to encourage them or to provide a word of wisdom and give them a key for their keychain.

Leadership can mean you're one of the first to volunteer and perform a task that gets a group on the right track toward reaching their goal.

Leaders sometimes lead without saying a single word; they just jump into a situation and take charge through their actions.

These are just a few ways that one can become a leader; there are thousands. Let's examine leadership from a scholarly point of view to see what's in it for you...

What is the definition of leadership? What is a leader and what does he or she do? And one of the bigger questions writers and thinkers ask: is leadership art or science?

The body of study on leadership pales in comparison to the research findings and literature available on the study of plants and animals; or oceans and mountains; or weather; or diseases and medicine.

Early study on the subject can be traced to about ninety years ago. Since then, thousands of books, master's theses and doctoral dissertations have been written on leadership. These works suggest several definitions of what leadership is, how it works and why this is so important.

Many have identified leadership by some common characteristics and traits of leaders, often using terms like "inspirational" or "charismatic". Others focus more on what leaders do rather than what they are. My personal favorite is that leadership is "influence".

Some mistakenly use terms to define leadership that are more applicable to management, not leadership. There's an important and critical distinction to make between management and leadership and a lot of people just plain miss it.

Management is not leadership. Leadership is not management. There is some overlap between the two disciplines but they are essentially two different things.

W.G. Bennis said that "managers are people who do things

right and leaders are people who do right things". This is not double talk; it actually sets out this important distinction.

Based on his research he said the differences were that...

managers administer	*leaders innovate*
managers maintain	*leaders develop*
managers control	*leaders inspire*
managers have a short-term view	*leaders have a long-term view*
managers ask how and when	*leaders ask what and why*
managers initiate	*leaders originate*
managers accept the status quo	*leaders challenge the status quo*

As the saying goes, anyone can steer a ship, but it takes a leader to chart the course. That's the difference...and it's a significant difference.

Don't get me wrong; every organization needs good managers and good management. I'm not putting management down...I'm just saying it is not a pillar of a tremendous life, personally or professionally. Steering a ship is an important part of life. In business, management lies at the core of how the enterprise gets things done.

In our personal lives, we need to manage a lot; our money, our time, our health, diet and physical fitness...and we need to plan everything from children and career and education to our golden years.

But these activities are steering a ship; the pillar of leadership is about plotting the course.

I believe management is more science than art and leadership is more art than science.

Max De Pree said, "leadership is much more an art, a belief, a condition of the heart than a set of things to do. The visible signs of artful leadership are expressed, ultimately, in its practice".

I've worked for companies and organizations that never came close to reaching their full potential because they believed too much in the science of management and did not put value in the art of leadership. What a shame.

It's difficult to grow and develop yourself much less the enterprise in an organization that is over-managed and under-led...

The almighty dollar can easily become more important than people. The company suffers from analysis paralysis. They fall prey to information paradox, the false belief that the more reports they can generate the better they can run the business.

People just don't stay very long in a company without true leadership. Worse yet, in the relentless search for profits and keeping shareholders and Wall Street analysts happy, some companies abandon ethics and become morally bankrupt.

As someone once said, "a company that just makes money is a poor company". Greed clouds judgment. People begin to feel defeated when they work for a company that's lost sight of its greatest asset: those who walk in every morning and out every evening on two feet.

John C. Maxwell talks about what happens when people sense defeat: he says they give as little as possible and look for excuses. They are tired, and they forsake the game plan. He also talks about what happens when people sense victory. He says they sacrifice to succeed, they look for ways to win and are energized, and they help team members.

To me, the difference in helping others sense victory over defeat is leadership.

Some people believe that leaders are born. I'm not convinced that's true. Maybe a few people are born with some raw genetic innate talent for leadership, but not many. I'm also not convinced that leaders are made. Some leadership skills can be learned and acquired. I believe the best leaders most likely have a combination of innate skills and learned skills...

That's been my experience in 35 years in the business world.

Learning is vital to leadership...and leaders never stop learning. They learn in the trenches of life. They learn through experience. They develop judgment and discernment. They learn how to speak up for the good of the enterprise or project or person. They learn how to assume responsibility and take the lead to get things done.

They learn to trust themselves...and others. They learn from their mistakes. They develop instincts about people and situations. And they acquire a lot of tremendous keys for their keychain.

Tremendous Howard loved telling the story about the nineteen year old who told his dad how amazed he was that his dad has such "good judgment" and that he always seemed to know what to do and that he always made the right decision.

The dad said, "thank you son". Then the son asked his dad how he learned about good judgment. The dad simply replied, "poor judgment". I can still see dad smiling with a twinkle in his eyes as he delivered that punchline. Then he'd tilt his head down a bit and say, "here endeth the lesson".

What he was talking about was experience and learning...things that are invaluable to a leader.

I believe you can become a leader if you're not one now...and if you already are a leader, you can always benefit from working to improve your leadership skills. These skills benefit you and, more importantly, those whom you lead.

They include exhibiting discipline of yourself physically, mentally, psychologically, spiritually, and financially; providing leadership within your family and among your friends and neighbors; and assuming leadership of projects and plans at work as well as in organizations to which you belong.

There's a lot of great information on leadership as it relates to traits and characteristics. I've included just a few of my favorites here.

As you read about Iacocca's C's of leadership, Maxwell's leadership traits and Baldoni's communication secrets of great leaders, you'll see applicability to leadership in your personal life as well as in your professional life.

You'll also clearly see why leadership is a pillar of a tremendous life. These are tremendous traits and characteristics and skills for which, as I said a few pages back, the world is crying and desperately needs.

Lee Iacocca, clearly one of the greatest business leaders of the last century, developed a "leadership template" to predict how good a president or CEO would be. Iacocca called the template his "C's of Leadership". "Nobody has them all," he said. Here's the template and some of his comments about them:

Curiosity
Listen to people outside the "Yes, sir" crowd. Read voraciously.
Creative
Go out on a limb. Leadership is all about managing change.
Communicate
A simple one. You should be talking to everybody, even your enemies.
Character
Having the guts to do the right thing. If you don't make it on character, the rest won't amount to much.
Courage
Courage in the 21st century doesn't mean posturing and bravado. Courage is a commitment to sit down at the negotiation table and talk. If you're a politician, courage means taking a position even when you know it will cost you votes.
Conviction
Fire in your belly. You've got to really want to get something done.
Charisma
The ability to inspire. People follow a leader because they trust him or her.
Competent
Surround yourself with people who know what they're doing. Be a problem solver.

Five Pillars of a Tremendous Life

Common sense
Your ability to reason.
Crisis
The biggest C is crisis. Leadership is forged in times of crisis. It's easy to sit there with your feet up on the desk and talk theory, or send someone else's kids off to war when you've never seen a battlefield yourself.

Iacocca's list of leadership traits is impressive. How many do you possess? If there are some traits you'd say you don't have today, can you work to acquire them? Some of them might seem to you to be a bit too difficult to acquire, like perhaps Creative or Charisma. I'd debate that with you...

I've seen people acquire some of the traits and skills Iacocca lists and their confidence rises dramatically and they acquire other leadership skills rapidly.

Don't sell yourself short.... there's more leadership in you than you think there is!

Perhaps the most visible skill leaders have is effective communication skills. John Kotter said, "without credible communication, and a lot of it, the hearts and minds of others will never be captured".

John Baldoni studied the "Communication Secrets of Great Leaders". He said that truly great leaders "communicate from within; roar for their people in supporting them; they communicate leading with hope; they have centered vision to their communication; that they use communication to promote new ideas to sell strategies; they are persistent in communicating all the time, and they live their message".

John C. Maxwell has developed a tremendous list of characteristics on leadership. They include some of Iacocca's, plus discernment, focus, generosity, initiative, listening, passion, and positive attitude, problemsolving, relationships, responsibility, security, self-discipline, servanthood, teachability, and vision.

To me, this is what leadership is, what leaders are and what leaders do...and that's why leadership is a pillar of a tremendous life.

Leaders take the responsibility to get things done. They create and drive change. They take calculated risks to help take enterprises and organizations as far as they can. Leaders set goals, they're disciplined and organized, they're on time, they accomplish much, and they make a positive difference.

I attended a conference on "growing your business" several years ago, and was given a one-pager that listed the ten qualities of a leader. The author is unknown. The qualities are well written and easy to understand. They clearly set out how you as a leader can "see" yourself...

The 10 Qualities of a Leader
Positive self-awareness; understanding where you are coming from
Positive self-esteem; liking yourself
Positive self-control; taking responsibility and making it happen
Positive self-motivation; wanting to and deciding you can
Positive self-expectancy; deciding to do better the next time
Positive self-image; seeing yourself changing and growing
Positive self-direction; having a game plan
Positive self-discipline; practicing mentally and thinking positively
Positive self-dimension; valuing yourself
Positive self-projection; reflecting yourself in how you walk, talk and listen.

Great leaders often become heroes. They have statues built to honor them. By the way, I've never seen a statue built to honor a manager.

I have a friend who says a major difference between leaders and managers is that mangers don't have to care but leaders do. Maybe that's why the statues are built...or not.

Leaders must also have compassion. Maxwell talks about leaders needing to touch a heart before asking for a hand. Woodrow Wilson said, "I do not believe that any man can lead who does not act under the impulse of a profound sympathy with those whom he leads".

As old-fashioned as some might say the word "virtue" is,

there's something else about leadership that makes it tremendous and a pillar of a tremendous life...great leaders for whom statues have been built often exhibited great virtue.

People respond to virtue because it's pure and right. Confucius said, "he who exercises government by means of his virtue may be compared to the north polar star, which keeps its place and all the stars turn towards it".

Virtuous...that term very much describes Tremendous Howard, Tremendous Charlie, Tremendous Mal, Tremendous Doug, and Tremendous Jimmy. They were all virtuous men of tremendous character who displayed the courage of conviction.

While all my heroes had tremendous virtues, I didn't idolize them nor did they want to be idolized. They were human beings with their own mistakes and misgivings and feet of clay. But they were virtuous.

Webster's New World College Dictionary defines virtue as moral excellence; right action and thinking; goodness or morality. This definition fits my heroes...and I bet it describes your heroes too. Virtue matters.

Indeed I've been blessed to know great men and women with virtue...and I've had countless leadership lessons...and I've been given so many leadership keys for my keychain. I've used my keys thousands of times with tremendous results. And so can you with your keys!

You'll find lots of keys when you start reading as much as you can about leadership. My favorite author on the topic is clearly John C. Maxwell. I think he's brilliant. I own just about every book he's written on leadership. I cannot recommend him and his works highly enough and suggest that you start your own John C. Maxwell collection soon.

Study the great leaders...political leaders, leaders from the worlds of business and industry, great men and women of faith, leaders who changed the face of history, tremendous women and men who did truly amazing things through their leadership.

Rev up the leadership of your life in new and better ways.

Build the characteristics of leadership from your heroes into your personal life.

In your professional life, take yourself and your company to higher plateaus of success by assuming the mantle of leadership. You'll be able to influence others and play a major role in their lives as you help them reach their goals and succeed.

You'll be able to overcome obstacles like never before; and you'll accomplish more than you thought you could. Your life will become tremendous and the lives of those you lead will become tremendous too.

"A leader is best when people barely know that he exists,
Not so good when people obey and acclaim him,
Worst of all when they despise him.
'Fail to honor people, they fail to honor you.'
But of a good leader, who talks little,
When his work is done, his aim fulfilled,
They will all say 'we did this ourselves'."
Lao Tzu

The Pillar of Encouragement

"Treat people as if they were what they
ought to be and you will help them to become
what they are capable of being."
Johann Wolfgang von Goethe

Encouragement is a truly amazing and tremendous thing. It is something we can easily do for others that affects their lives in very positive ways. John C. Maxwell talks about encouragement being the oxygen of the soul.

It's also the gasoline for the engine of human effort and human spirit. Encouragement can move people to think differently, to act differently and to accomplish a lot.

Encouragement is like a drug, a good one, one that can positively affect the human psyche and the human will.

Encouraging a child or a family member or a co-worker or a friend is incredibly powerful. Perhaps you're one of the fortunate people who've had great encouragers in your life. If so, you know how truly powerful encouragement is.

And yet...most of us seldom encourage others. Why is this so? If encouragement is so tremendous and so powerful, doesn't it make sense that we would want to do it a lot more often? Of course it does.

I can only guess why we don't encourage others more... maybe it has something to do with how much we have or, in this case, have not been encouraged by others. Or maybe we let negativity creep in and hold us back.

I once heard a clinical psychologist discuss negativity and its effects. She said that on average, seven out of every ten thoughts human beings have are negative thoughts. Wow… 70% of our thoughts are, on average, negative.

We sure can discourage each other, can't we? We've all seen it; at gatherings by the water cooler at work, or at the bar after work…whiners and losers congregating to complain and drag everybody down with them.

It's a tough and often unforgiving world. We can easily be beaten up, let down, put down, and become dejected and disappointed. We can become discouraged and start to think we can't win or we can't succeed. It can become a downward spiral so easily and so quickly.

On the other hand, most of us respond to encouragement positively. The effects can be dramatic.

There's an old saying that sums it up nicely: "as we think, we do". True. I'd add that "as we're encouraged, we think…and often do!"

I've had coaches tell me and my teammates, "if you think you're beat, you are". And I've had coaches who said, "we're going to win". I don't have to tell you which coaches were the better ones.

The worst coach I ever had did the worst thing I ever saw a coach do. This is a true story. I'm not making it up. Believe me, it actually happened. I was there and I'll never forget it…

Our team was beating our competition badly in a game where we were the clear underdogs. It was their Homecoming Game on their home field. We had only a handful of our fans there….and they were going crazy with our amazing success…while the large home team crowd was deadly silent.

At half-time, we were ahead by the unbelievable score of 27 to 0. Everything we tried on offense and defense worked… everything they tried failed. We scored with ease. I remember being "in a zone" that you've probably heard athletes talk about…it was fantastic…and playing seemed almost effortless.

We came into the locker room at half-time hooting and hollering at the top of our voices, pounding on the lockers and on each other, and giving each other a lot of high fives. Our coach had a choice of what to say to us.

He made the wrong choice...the worst possible choice.

He could have told us we were great; that we were playing so well we could beat any team on the planet; that he was proud of us; that we should rest up because we were going to go out there in the second half and beat them by such an outlandish score that the world would take note...or something to that effect.

He could have been so encouraging...and we would've hung on every positive and reaffirming word of praise. And we would have believed him. But he didn't say any of those things. He said something else...

He told us that the other team was really good; that we were very lucky to have such a lead; that they would come out all fired-up since it was their Homecoming...and he believed they could make a comeback.

And they did.

The better they played, the worse we played. They got faster; we got slower. Their heads were up...ours were down. Everything worked for them; nothing worked for us. And when the final whistle blew, we had lost the game by the score of 30 to 27.

We were stunned. We could hardly summon the strength to walk off the field. I think about that game every so often. The experience is so real to me and is so clear, it seems like it happened just yesterday...and yet it happened 37 years ago.

It was the most painful lesson I ever learned in discouragement.

We can never get enough encouragement from others. We all need more encouraging. Maybe we need to be better trained to do so or maybe we've not had enough role models in the area of encouragement.

Whatever the reasons, they're not good enough for me. I think you'd agree the world could be a better place if we were encouraging each other more often. It's got to be better to be lifting each other up instead of tearing each other down.

I believe encouragement is a pillar of a tremendous life because it makes other people's lives better with a few well-placed words. Plus, encouraging others affects us, the encouragers, in very positive ways.

We know we've helped…we've lightened someone's load a bit…we've given them support and helped them find the inner strength to carry on and accomplish whatever they've set out to do.

From children's literature to real life dramas, we've all been moved by great stories with positive outcomes…

The Little Engine That Could, by saying to itself, "I think I can, I think I can" to get up the steep hill; and then, "I thought I could, I thought I could" after it did…

The sports teams that played unselfishly and as a real team and believed they could win…then won championships despite great obstacles and odds…

The troops in combat that turned the tide from certain defeat and death to glorious victory after it appeared all was lost and they didn't stand a chance…

Organizations about to go out of business that experience an unbelievable and positive transformation in order to achieve an astounding turn-around and comeback…

Marriages about to fail that are miraculously saved and renewed because hearts were changed and pride was overcome and forgiveness was given…

People who have fallen prey to a nasty addiction and all sorts of evil…who triumph and get healthy and conquer their demons and go on to lead tremendous lives...

Great stories of people who received encouragement and discovered extra strength and resolve to win.

I know many such true stories…you do too. People who were encouraged…and encouraged others not to give up or give in or quit; to believe; and to try again. As trite as some may think the old saying may sound, it's true: "If You Can Believe It You Can Achieve It".

Reading and sharing great stories about success is encouraging. It's encouraging to learn about how people positively changed themselves, and then positively changed their situation to bring about tremendous results.

Sharing stories about great people, great events or great ideas and moments in history is encouraging. Encouragement is tremendous...and is its own reward.

Encouragement can lift people out of self-doubt. It can help them believe in themselves for the first time...or maybe believe in themselves again if they've lost confidence and are second-guessing themselves...

It's a great feeling to know that someone else is encouraging you and is on your side...that they are in your corner; rooting for you; and they believe you can win..

It's tremendous to know that others are encouraging you to get to higher places in life; to complete that project or course of study or that degree; to make the most of that relationship; to go for that promotion or new position in the company; to change your career path; to pursue your passion and purpose; to have a deeper and fuller and more rewarding life.

It's not difficult to be an encourager. It's rewarding; and everybody wins, as Jim Stovall points out in his quote at the end of this chapter.

People who are encouragers have tremendous attitudes, high energy, a lot of optimism, loads of enthusiasm and confidence.

Tremendous Howard and Tremendous Barbara were great encouragers to me. They supported everything I did in school and sports...and every major decision I made in my career.

Tremendous Charlie was not only a big encourager in my life...he *taught* encouragement. He exhorted others for decades to "be an encourager". He loved to talk about the Apostle Paul as the shining example of an encourager.

Tremendous Mal and Doug were tactical encouragers. They

encouraged me on how to play ball or how to make music; how to get better; how to study; what to focus on; how to be my best.

Coach Mal would look at me from the other side of the football field and raise his fist in a sweeping action from his right knee to his left shoulder with a big smile and he'd shout "you can do it big guy". With his encouragement, I believed I could. And I did.

Tremendous Jimmy encouraged me from my early adult to mid-life years in how to manage my finances, my career, and my post-graduate education.

Tremendous Howard and Barbara, Tremendous Charlie and Tremendous Mal were committed Christians who encouraged me to grow in my faith.

I've added all the keys my heroes gave me to my keychain and I've tried my best to pay it forward; to be an encourager to my siblings, children, grandchildren, teammates, colleagues, friends and neighbors.

I love encouraging movies, books, and music...and often give them as gifts. People love them and sometimes get copies to give to others. Encouragement is one of those things that can spread quickly when people learn how great it is, how easy it is to do, and what great things it does.

Every time I hear Josh Groban sing "You Raise Me Up" or Bette Midler sing "Wind Beneath My Wings" or Simon and Garfunkel sing "Bridge Over Troubled Water" or James Taylor or Carole King sing "You've Got a Friend" I get emotional because the words are so tremendous...they remind me of my heroes and what they did to encourage me.

I love being around encouraging people. We feed off of each other and the synergy flows. We laugh a lot and we smile a lot...we nod our heads in agreement a lot and we are strengthened and renewed.

And I love encouraging others and making them more confident of their own talents and abilities. It's tremendous to encourage someone then see them win and accomplish their goals. William Arthur Ward said, "Flatter me, and I may not believe you. Criticize me, and I may not like you. Ignore me, and I may not forgive you. But encourage me, and I may not forget you".

There are two other great quotes I use quite often in business that set out why encouragement is such a positive and powerful thing...

The first is from Maya Angelou who said, "people will forget what you said, and people will forget what you did, but people will never forget how you made them feel".

The second quote is from Alex F. Osborn, who said that "creativity is so delicate a flower that praise tends to make it bloom, while discouragement often nips it in the bud...any of us will put out more and better ideas if our efforts are appreciated".

Hopefully, you've been encouraged countless times and have had tremendous encouragers in your life. What keys did they give you for your keychain? What encouraging things have you done for others?

There's no excuse for us to not encourage each other more and more often. In fact, there are lots of great reasons why we should be *more* encouraging to others.

Be an encourager. Be others' number one fan. Tell others you believe in them and that they'll win. It will do so much for them and so much for you.

"You need to be aware of what others are doing, applaud their efforts, acknowledge their successes, and encourage them in their pursuits. When we all help one another, everybody wins."
Jim Stovall

The Pillar of Faith

"Faith is the opening of all sides and at every
level of one's life to the divine inflow."
Martin Luther King, Jr.

Faith, and by that I mean spiritual faith, is a very personal thing. What faith means to me and how I bring my faith to life is unique for me. A few chapters ago I shared that I'm a Christian. I have been since my youth and my faith matters the most in helping make my life a tremendous life.

How about you? What does the term spiritual faith mean to you? Would you say you are a person of faith? If so, how do you "live" your faith? Would you say your faith is an important part of your life?

If someone tells me they have little or no faith...or that they've lost their faith, I believe they're one pillar shy of a tremendous life. That's a bold statement, and I say it with conviction. Here's why...

For me, faith provides answers to such fundamental questions as why I'm here and how I got here; where I'm headed...and how to get there. God's love and faithfulness to us brings us comfort in time of sorrow and pain; an inner peace about every aspect and event of our lives; a knowledge that God will be with us always.

What could possibly matter more than that?

When Hans Kung talked about why he wrote the book *On Being a Christian*, he said the book "was written not because the author thinks he is a good Christian, but because being a Christian was a particularly good thing". I agree.

61

Five Pillars of a Tremendous Life

I strive to be Christlike in my personal and professional lives. That's setting the bar high, but it's my way to show that I'm a follower of Christ. This does not make me better than anyone else; not for one minute. And I'm anything but "holier than thou".

I'm serious about my faith, and I seek God's will. I want to be used by God and be faithful to God. But I don't claim to have "arrived"...my faith is a journey.

Tremendous Charlie had a great way of saying this. He'd often say, "I'm not what I ought to be, I'm not what I thought I'd be, I'm not what I hoped I'd be...but by the grace of God, I'm not what I was". Amen to that!

What Charlie was talking about was this process of learning and growing in faith. He acknowledged he was a changed person but that he too was on a journey.

So did Tremendous Howard and Barbara. The same goes for me and for you. We all have feet of clay; all the more reason to seek God's will and an ever-deepening and abiding faith.

One of the tremendous things my faith has taught me to do is to live life Inside Out. Jesus said the second greatest commandment was to love your neighbor as much as you love yourself.

He said the greatest commandment was to love the Lord your God with all of your heart and with all of your soul and with all of your mind. He said the second greatest commandment was like the first...and that the Law and the writings of the Prophets hung on these two commandments.

You see, Jesus knew how much we love ourselves: a lot; usually too much if we're honest with ourselves. In attempting to follow the second greatest commandment, we shift the focus from ourselves to others. And then everything changes...I mean *everything*. There's no place in our lives for selfishness. We become givers more than takers.

Givers find purpose in their lives. They assume the mantle of leadership more often than not. They are great encouragers.

And they're often overflowing with love for others. There you have it; all five pillars of a tremendous life…each one an outpouring of faith.

My experience has been that people with faith in God view life differently. They're recognized for their capacity to forgive and for their compassion. In fact, they're so different that people notice it…and often ask why.

I've been asked what makes me so "different" on many occasions. It wasn't necessarily because I talked about God or Christ or quoted the Bible. It was because others could sense something different in me…about what I said and the way I said it and about the way I treated others.

I believe what they saw was the love of Christ at work through me. Maybe they didn't actually know it as that, but that's what it was.

I genuinely and unconditionally love others. Tremendous Barbara taught me that more than anyone else did. Loving others and giving to them and serving them are examples of how I live my faith. I've been blessed to receive this kind of love and to see this kind of faith in my heroes.

And while my heroes' beliefs may have been similar to mine, I've also seen genuine love and tremendous faith at work in people whose beliefs are not the same as mine.

Many people claim membership in an organized religion and yet they exhibit little or no real faith. On the other hand, many people have deep spiritual faith but don't call any particular religion home.

It's not about what religious group a person belongs to…it's about what they believe and how their faith resonates through their lives. I'm open-minded on the subject of different faiths. While I may be more tolerant of other's beliefs, it has never altered what I believe.

I'll debate differences in beliefs and faith, but I won't argue over them; to me, debating is an exchange of intelligence…arguing is an exchange of ignorance. I believe showing respect for others' beliefs is a healthy way to create an environment where I have the opportunity to share what I believe and why.

Tremendous Charlie put the topic of showing respect for other faiths in understandable and clear terms. He'd say, "I don't know what works for you, but for me it's the Gospel according to John, Chapter 3, verse 16".

Then he'd go on to quote it in his very loving tone of voice and with a very warm and loving smile…"For God so loved the world he gave His only begotten Son, that whosoever believeth in Him shall not perish but have eternal life".

What a loving and clear way to be accommodating and understanding of others yet letting them know exactly where he stood.

Tremendous Howard knew about my tolerance of other faiths. It never bothered him. I had his blessing to form my own opinions on matters of faith even if they were different than his or mom's opinions. I didn't need his okay, but I sure liked having it.

I remember him smiling broadly as he'd turn to mom whenever the three of us talked about our differences, which by the way, we always considered to be relatively minor. He'd pat mom on the knee and say, "Honey, David's all right; he just wants to have communion with all the saints!"…then he'd get that special gleam in his eyes.

My faith is about deeply held beliefs and personal experiences that have come to me through my relationship with the God of the Bible. I believe that this relationship was made available to me through the finished work of Christ.

I have a truly abundant life. Not abundant in terms of money and possessions and power and fame…abundant in things money cannot buy; contentment and joy and peace.

If you don't have faith in your life, I encourage you to ask the people in your life, in your neighborhood, at work or at school, about their faith. It's a great place to start.

You might think I'm crazy to suggest that. I know we were taught to "never bring up the topics of religion or politics" in social or business settings because these topics might offend others.

Well, okay then; don't talk about "religion" since that word has connotations about certain groups and sects. Talk about faith. That isn't semantics to me. I've always believed spiritual faith and religion are two different things.

Ask people to share what they believe. I think you'll be surprised at how willing they are to open up and how comfortable they are to talk about their faith.

When I've done that, I respectfully listen to what others say. Some believe, in general, as I do; others believe quite differently.

I've always enjoyed opportunities to share what I believe and why I believe it as well as to listen to others as they talk about differences in their faith from mine. I've never had anyone tell me they're offended or uncomfortable with our conversations.

I'm convinced a real void exists in the lives of many people…and that there's a deep inner longing in many people's lives to know God. And I believe that's why so many people want to talk about the subject of faith.

Of course, it can be uncomfortable when someone wears their beliefs "on their sleeve" and they try to convert you to their way of thinking by hitting you over the head with a baseball bat. Well not literally…but you know what I mean.

It's important to be able to tell the difference between what I heard a pastor once say was either "spiritual fervor" or "emotional fever". I'm in favor of the former and not much of a fan of the latter.

Tremendous Howard loved telling the story about the pastor who was overheard complaining that some of the well-intentioned folks in the church were "so Heavenly minded they were no Earthly good".

For me, spiritual faith is about being Earthly good. Faith

provides real and practical answers and comfort in times of sorrow, disappointment, heartbreak, and loss…as well as joy in times of celebration and happiness.

Faith is a gift. Carl Jung said that "faith cannot be made; it is in the truest sense a gift of grace". The gift of faith is certainly one of life's most precious gifts because it's a gift that never stops giving.

Faith doesn't always provide easy and quick answers, and sometimes it's hard to comprehend the balance between God's will and the free will granted to us.

It's not easy for me to explain how God can give us the "peace that passes all understanding"…and I'm probably not doing a very good job of it. But maybe I don't need to. An often used saying in our family comes to mind…

Tremendous Barbara learned this saying during the Second World War from a dear old African-American woman named Hattie who worked for the wealthy family next door. Mom was the beautiful young wife of a U.S. Army Air Force pilot, handsome young Tremendous Howard, and they had a beautiful new baby girl, Tremendous Carol.

Whenever Hattie and mom would meet each other at the clothesline in the backyard, mom got a few free slices of life from Hattie. Sometimes it was advice; sometimes it was to share an experience from Hattie's life.

Mom said these tidbits from Hattie were tremendous. They must have been; Tremendous Barbara is 87 years old now and she still smiles lovingly when any of the four of us children mention Hattie's name.

One of Hattie's sayings has become a part of our family culture. We use the phrase quite often. It seems to me the saying applies as I struggle to find the right words to explain the wonder and beauty of faith.

If Hattie talked about something that had happened to her or was trying to express a thought but just couldn't find the words to explain it, she'd say, "oh, Miss Barbara, its better felt than 'telt'".

Mohandas K. Gandhi said, "faith does not contradict reason but transcends it". The writer of the Book of Hebrews said that "faith is the substance of things hoped for, the evidence of things not seen".

The faith I've developed during my life came from teaching, studying, prayer, worship, and fellowship with others. And my faith has grown through real life experiences…and through life's failures and successes.

I've been challenged to keep my faith when I've seen bad things happen to good people and good things happen to bad people.

I've been touched by God when performing sacred music, whether it was in America's best concert halls or in churches in several countries.

My faith has been strengthened by seeing first-hand how life was anything but tremendous for others who had no faith, and how I could help them as a servant of God.

You've known or seen people who've lost hope; people who were used by others and discarded as though they were yesterday's rubbish…

Perhaps you've known people who walked away from their faith as a result of circumstances, pain, disappointment and disillusionment. Their lives become driven by bitterness and false pride or a "hardened heart" as the saying goes.

I always pray that these people will give faith a chance…or as the case may be, another chance. God works in mysterious ways. Not hocus-pocus mysterious ways; tremendously mysterious ways in a sense that we cannot fully understand and must take on faith.

Jesus said if someone had faith the size of a mustard seed, he or she could move a mountain. The average mustard seed is about the size of the space inside the number "zero" on a standard computer keyboard. Jesus made it perfectly clear that a little faith goes a very, very long way.

I recently read an excellent new book called *Why Faith*

Five Pillars of a Tremendous Life

Matters, by Rabbi David J. Wolpe. The foreword was written by Rick Warren, a well-known Christian pastor. I recommend the book to you as a tremendous contemporary treatise on faith and the search for truth and meaning in today's world.

I also recommend you talk about faith with friends and family. Discover where God plans to take you on your journey to faith. Talk to God too. The Bible says fervent prayer avails much. It does.

Mitch Albom said, "There is a fullness of life with faith and an emptiness of life without it".

What God can and will do for you, and what God can do for others through you and your faith, will be tremendous.

"Faith leads us beyond ourselves.
It leads us directly to God."
Pope John Paul II

The Pillar of Love

"What the world needs now is love, sweet love...
It's the only thing that there's just too little of.
What the world needs now is love, sweet love...
No, not just for some, oh, but just for everyone."
Burt Bacharach

What an interesting word "love" is in the English language, and how many ways we use it...

When I think of love, my immediate thoughts are of how much I love Tremendous Debbie. Then, of course, I think about my family and then my very close and dear friends.

Yet I also claim that I love spring and autumn. I love riding my old bicycle. And I love the life insurance industry.

I also love the Minnesota Vikings and the Minnesota Twins and the Los Angeles Lakers. I love a good steak grilled "Pittsburgh rare"...especially at Morton's of Chicago, a restaurant chain I love. And I love New Zealand white wine. And I love baroque music.

I'll spare you a long list of the things I say I love. I think the "things" I say I love might be better placed in a category of things I very strongly like.

The love that's tremendous and is "real love" is the love we have for others and the love we receive from others. This could well be romantic love, and it should be. But it can also be some other types of love we have for others.

Whom do you love? Who loves you? I encourage you to make a list of the people you genuinely love and those who love you. I think you'll find making the list a good exercise...

Five Pillars of a Tremendous Life

It'll probably tell you, and others with whom you're willing to share your list, a lot about you, about your purpose in life, and about who some of your heroes are. It will also likely provide insight into how the pillars of your tremendous life have been built or are being built.

An unconditional and unabashed and unending love for others plays a major role in making them content and truly happy. And a loving person's attitude and behavior affects others in tremendous ways.

The heroes of movies and literature often exhibit a deep love for others or for causes that are right and just. The villains are just the opposite; they are greedy and selfish...and some are even downright wicked and evil. The only love they usually have is for themselves.

If you didn't notice on my list, there's no reference to material things like money or jewelry and cars and houses or boats or planes. I've never known anyone who counted material possessions as a central part of what made their lives tremendous. Convenient and luxurious maybe, but not tremendous.

I give materialism and consumerism a failing grade for misleading marketing. In the 1980's, a popular bumper sticker said, "the one who dies with the most toys wins". What a cruel hoax. The truth is the one with the most toys when he dies...still dies.

I also give a failing grade to movies and television for often portraying something as love that is not love at all: lust. Love is not lust. Lust is not love. Oh that the world could learn this!

So if love, real genuine authentic love is a pillar of a tremendous life, what kind of love is that? For starters, let's consider the attributes of love identified by the Apostle Paul in the New Testament, First Corinthians, Chapter 13.

Paul's definition of love comes from the Greek word "agape". Agape love is sometimes described as divine love, unconditional love, pro-active love, and sacrificing love.

Writing about this kind of genuine love, Paul wrote, "Love is patient and kind; love is not jealous or boastful; it is not arrogant or rude. Love does not insist on its own way; it is not irritable or resentful; it does not rejoice at wrong, but rejoices in the right. Love bears all things, believes all things, hopes all things".

Kahlil Gibran said, "when you love you should not say God is in my heart, but rather, I am in the heart of God. And think not you can direct the course of love, for love, if it finds you worthy, directs your course". Now that's love!

I saw Tremendous Howard and Tremendous Barbara love each other with this kind of love…every day. Speaking of dad and mom…

I'd say one of the expressions of love I'm talking about is the true love that makes two people one in marriage. I'm convinced love in marriage is second only to the love of God…and to me, these two types of love are among the most tremendous.

Another tremendous love is what we call familial love and brotherly love. This kind of love is well-defined in what I call the trusty old dictionary I keep in my office: a profoundly tender and passionate affection for another…a feeling of warm personal attachment or deep affection…and affectionate concern for the well-being of others.

Next to my trusty old dictionary is my trusty old thesaurus. It lists additional terms I'd use to describe the love we can have for friends, family, and others including devotion, adoration, affectionate regard, sentiment, esteem, admiration, brotherhood or sisterhood, compatibility, sympathy, and cordiality.

This is the kind of love that we see at work in families and on teams and in schools and places of worship and neighborhoods. I wish there was more of this kind of love between nations!

Unfortunately, we seldom see this kind of love in business and in corporations…and I've always believed that's sad. If more heads of companies would drop their bravado and misguided focus on numbers and replace it with a genuine love for their people, I think they'd get their numbers and their growth and their profitability.

A tremendous champion of love in the marketplace was Herb Kelleher when he was CEO of Southwest Airlines. This tremendous airline is even called the LUV airline. You probably know the Southwest story, but if you don't, I suggest you read about it…it's amazing.

I wish we could get more love into business, but we'd have to shift away from keeping Wall Street analysts and stockholders happy with the results of the last quarter. That would take courage. Unfortunately, most business leaders and corporations just don't have much courage.

Genuine love is unique. It borrows some of Tremendous Charlie's "give to give…don't give to get" philosophy. Genuine love loves with no expectation, no "trading" as Charlie said that "giving to get" was. There is no quid pro quo. As Oscar Wilde put it, "the aim of love is to love; no more, and no less".

People who genuinely love others have character traits that are usually easy to see in almost everything they say and do. They're full of gratitude. Their lives are in balance. They're accepting and tolerant. And they possess one of life's greatest treasures, the ability to forgive.

People with love show it. You see it in their smiles and their eyes. You hear it in their tones of voices and their laughter. You sense it in the words they choose to express themselves and how they feel about others.

People who are loved respond to being loved. It makes them happier…they have a spring in their step. I'm no physician or scientist, but it has always appeared quite evident to me that people who love and are loved are healthier physically, emotionally, psychologically, spiritually, and mentally.

One of the things I really like about most people who genuinely love others is that they can say "I love you" openly and often. There is no room for stoicism in love. The old line about "well, I don't have to actually tell you I love you…you know I do" is a bunch of bunk! Yes you *do* have to tell others you love them. They want to hear it. Don't you?

To some people, loving others and letting them know it...actually saying "I love you"...seems difficult or risky. Maybe that's because we've been hurt in the past or maybe we've been taught that showing emotions was a form of weakness.

Indeed it is risky to open yourself up and be vulnerable. But I think it's worse to be so safe that you never experience the wonder and joy and benefits of loving others and letting them love you.

Benjamin Franklin said, "If you would be loved, love and be lovable". He was right...and an important part of loving and being lovable is to say it.

I tell Tremendous Debbie and my kids and grandkids that I love them every chance I get. It's always, and I mean *always*, the last thing I say to them in telephone conversations and e-mails. The same goes for my mom, Debbie's mom, our brothers and sisters, and our extended family.

Why? Because we all know that life is precious and it can end in a second. We never know when that time is coming. There is no promise we'll see tomorrow. So in case I'm gone tomorrow, they can remember the last thing I said to them was "I love you".

Oh, how very much I love my tremendous family!

And I love my many dear friends. What a blessing it is that these people love me back! We share a strong bond and we take comfort in knowing we can count on each other no matter what. We thoroughly enjoy sharing each others' joys and burdens.

I count the total and unconditional love I received from Tremendous Howard and Barbara and from Tremendous Charlie, Mal, Doug, and Jimmy among the greatest gifts I ever received.

I have such tremendous memories of feeling loved by my grandparents and teachers and coaches and friends and fellow-students and teammates.

My mentors and family members love and have loved me in

their own special way. What I received from their loving me and how I have benefited from their love are things that I cannot put into words. It's better felt than 'telt'!

Victor Hugo said, "what a grand thing, to be loved! What a grander thing still, to love".

The lyrics of so many popular songs over time have focused on love. Everyone has their favorites. Mine include the Beatles' "All You Need is Love", Paul Stookey's "Wedding Song" and many, many more.

Irving Berlin wrote so many wonderful songs about true love. So did George and Ira Gershwin. Their song "Someone to Watch Over Me" is my all-time favorite. Tremendous Barbara loves it too...tears of joy stream down her cheeks when she hears it, thinking about her 67 years with Tremendous Howard. I cry when she cries...it's tremendous!

Real true love as set out in First Corinthians is exactly what the world needs. We don't need any more lust, greed, selfishness, pride, war; or endless cycles of violence and hunger and poverty, or hatred and bigotry.

We need love. Real love. Sweet love. Not just for some...but or everyone. If we loved each other more, we'd understand each other better...and have more respect for each other. And we'd help and support each other more.

No matter what kind of love it is...for God, spouse or partner, child, grandchild, parent or grandparent, brother or sister, neighbor, colleague, teammate, or friend...we need it...we need to give it and we need to receive it.

Whether we're giving and showing our love to others or receiving it from them, there's something about it that is better felt than 'telt'. It makes us happy. It makes us content. We know we're needed and wanted and appreciated. It uplifts our spirit and our attitude and it shows in our behavior.

There's so much to be said about love and what it can do. It is a common thread woven through all the pillars of a tremendous life.

David F. Pierce

Love is at the very center of purpose. You cannot be a fully-functioning leader without a real love for the enterprise and for the people you lead. The main reason you encourage others is because you love them and want to see them succeed. And faith is all about love...the love of God...the love *for* God...and sharing God's love with others.

When you love someone, there is no burden too heavy, no sacrifice too great, no problem too big, no price too high. Love is like the morning sun after the long dark night. It's like spring following a cold, hard, bitter winter.

I bet you know that. Because if you've been truly loved and if you've loved others, then you know how wonderful love is. We can never get enough love...and we can never give enough love. There's no doubt about it...love is tremendous!

"I am a little pencil in the hand of a writing God who is sending a love letter to the world."
Mother Teresa

Tone of Life

"The essence of life is to care...
the secret of life is to dare...
the adventure of life is to learn...
the challenge of life is to change...
the joy of life is to love."
Anonymous

It's been said that 90% of the world's tensions could be eased by changing just one thing...tone of voice.

Understanding and cooperation usually result from communicating with a tone of voice that is pleasant and gentle, when we talk in a caring and considerate manner, when we show respect and kindness.

I think we can apply the tone of voice principle to the way we live our lives. I like to call it the *Tone of Life*. It's about how we talk, how we think, what's important to us, what our attitude is, what we do, how we do it, how we act and how we react.

Two examples of a tremendous tone of life can be found in Appendix D and Appendix E. Robert Louis Stevenson and Kent Keith have each, in their own way, expressed the best way to approach life and to develop a tone of life.

In their writings you'll find many keys to happiness and contentment. I give printed copies of their writings to people all the time. Everybody reads them and quietly nods in agreement. I bet you will too.

Martha Washington wrote, "I am determined to be cheerful and happy in whatever situation I find myself. For I have learned that the greater part of our misery or unhappiness is

determined not by our circumstance but by our disposition".
She was obviously talking about having a positive tone of life.

Earlier I quoted Charles Swindoll, who commented on the
attributes of having the right attitude. It's worth repeating: he
said that life was 10% what happens to you and 90% how you
react to it. Tone of Life.

In this book, we've considered the tremendous results we
can realize in our lives and help create in the lives of others
when we:

Find purpose and take action to accomplish it
Develop leadership and become accountable and responsible
Encourage others and lift them up
Have faith to keep us grounded…and
Love others and tell them so.

I saw the results, and a tremendous tone of life in
Tremendous Charlie, Tremendous Howard, and the other truly
tremendous people I've written about in this book.

They were shining examples of the five pillars coming to
life. They showed the way to me and I am forever grateful they
did.

It was their purpose, different as it was for each of them, that
made them great. Their commitment to their purpose was
unwavering.

It was their leadership of me and my siblings, my friends
and my classmates, my teammates and my co-workers that
made them great.

It was their encouragement in word and deed and thought
and many supportive ways that helped me believe in myself
and in my skills and in my abilities.

It was their faith in God that brought them truth, wisdom
and salvation.

It was their love that made them fully human and brought
them into caring relationships.

Five Pillars of a Tremendous Life

It was their gentle yet firm hand...directing me...pointing out the way...lighting the path...asking rather than telling...correcting only when necessary.

It was their smile and their hugs. It was in their voice. It was in their written notes, letters, and e-mails. It was their thankfulness. It was their contentment. It was their gifts. It was their keys.

It was their tone of life.

These tremendous people taught me how to be thankful; to be humble; to put others first; to live Inside Out, to pay it forward, to discover purpose, to lead, to encourage others, to have faith, and to love.

Their lessons helped me develop and shape my own tone of life. With their teaching and my learning, I was prepared for whatever came my way in life...whether it be opportunity or hardship.

Sometimes we fool ourselves into thinking we can control and plan everything in our lives. We can control some events and activities...but as John Lennon wrote, "life is what happens to you while you're busy making other plans". He was right.

That's why Swindoll's 90% is so important. That's why having a tone of life built on the five pillars is so important...and so tremendous.

The five pillars, however you apply them, serve as the foundation and support for living life with confidence. And it's a tremendous thing to live life confidently. To live in confidence means you have conquered fear. It also means your life is not hindered by needless worry.

My heroes didn't worry about the future and what it held. They didn't worry or have any fear about financial ruin, poor health, or the things so many people worry about...needlessly. Nor did they worry about death.

In fact, my heroes taught me that the only way to live life to the fullest was to have a healthy and rational openness to the fact and the truth that death comes to us all. Not one of them feared death, nor do I. Their life lessons included teaching me how to die...

Tremendous Howard turned eighty years old on September 10, 2001...the day before a group of terrorists shocked the world with acts of unspeakable violence towards innocent people in New York City, at the Pentagon, and in Shanksville, Pennsylvania.

Two and a half weeks later, he lost his battle to cancer. He immediately stepped on shore in Heaven and found it Home.

A few weeks earlier, the family gathered to say good-bye to dad. What a joyous time it was. Joyous? Yes...but still difficult. We didn't gather to mourn dad's imminent death. We were there to celebrate his tremendous life, to thank him for all he did for each one of us...and to love him right up until it was time to say good-bye.

All four of us kids were taught from an early age that death was part of life...that we should accept it...that it was right and prudent to be ready for it in the twinkling of an eye.

My first lesson in life insurance came from dad, who had plenty of it for his young family way back in the 1940s. He had made the arrangements for his family financially. He had also prepared for death at any stage of his life mentally, spiritually, and in every other way.

How well I recall holding Dad's hand, praying with him, thanking him for everything, telling him how very much I loved him, how happy I was that he loved me, kissing him on the lips, saying "good-bye dad", then turning away to lock in the memory of this moment...our last time together in this life.

Tremendous Jimmy died just 43 days later. I had the chance to say good-bye to him too, but in a very different way. He and I had agreed way back in 1981 that we'd never say good-bye but instead would say "see you later" whenever we parted company.

We honored that agreement for over twenty years...until

Debbie and I visited an aging and ailing Jimmy in retirement in Phoenix.

It was easy to see his health was deteriorating rapidly. We talked about it and he said he was ready to go...that he'd had a long, successful, and wonderful life. Indeed he had. So I shouldn't have been caught by surprise when he took us to the airport at the end of our visit...but I was.

We got to the airport and Jimmy hugged Debbie, kissed her, and told her he loved her. Then he turned to me...gave me one of his famous big bear hugs...and kissed me on the cheek, pressing very hard. He held me at arm's length just like Tremendous Charlie always did...he looked me straight in the eye, smiled and said, "good-bye, Davey".

I said, "good-bye, Jimmy...thanks for everything...I love you". He said "I love you too" then he turned away, got in his car and drove away. Debbie and I walked into the airport terminal. She turned and saw that I was smiling a big smile but also wiping tears from my eyes.

She asked if I was all right. I said I was, but that we'd seen Jimmy for the last time. I told her for the first and only time, Jimmy just said good-bye. Then I told her about our agreement. Jimmy died a few weeks later.

It was tough to have my dad and then Jimmy die within a span of six weeks. But in truth, they're with me every day...and I meet them in what Jimmy called "the close corner" of my brain.

He used to say, "Davey, after I'm gone, just close your eyes and go to that close corner of your brain; there I will meet you and there I will greet you". And he does.

Seven years later it was time to say good-bye to Tremendous Charlie.

He and I had stayed in weekly contact since he came to New Zealand a few months earlier and brought the house down with his humor, his wisdom, his love, his testimony, and the fulfillment of his promise to never quit.

We talked about the documentary. He said he knew it would

be tremendous. And we talked about the past. We talked about so many memories.

His voice got weaker and weaker; and he talked slower and lower every time I called. Then came the call that was to be the last...but it didn't start out that way.

I thanked him for the books he'd sent that had just arrived...and we talked about the life insurance industry. The longer we were on the phone, the more rapidly he tired.

Then he said in a very, very weak whisper, "my Beloved, the doctor says I get to go Home in about seven days. I can't tell you how excited I am".

Even though his whisper still had that old Charlie Jones lift and emphasis when he said "ex-cited"...his next sentence faded off and I couldn't make out what he said. Instead, I could hear other voices in the background. I knew it was time...

I said, "Charlie...this will be the last time we talk this side of Heaven. I'll get out of the way now and let you spend time with your tremendous family. All I can think to say to you just now is thank you, thank you, thank you. I love you". He replied, "oh my Beloved...I'm so proud of you! Thank you, David... I love you too. Good-bye".

I just barely whispered "good-bye, Charlie"...tears of thankfulness and love and joy streaming down my face.

I hung up the phone and thought, in full Charles "Tremendous" Jones intonation of course, how about that? Two guys with a rich history of shouting and hollering and slapping our hands together and kicking in the air...and here we are both just barely whispering as we say good-bye. It was tremendous.

I've been blessed to have great people in my life: a tremendous wife; tremendous children and grandchildren; tremendous parents; a tremendous family; tremendous teachers and coaches; tremendous business partners; tremendous teammates; tremendous friends.

Their tone of life was just as tremendous as they were and are...sweet, loving, caring, forgiving, encouraging, inclusive, and tender. Their fingerprints are all over my life.

The number of lessons I learned from them about life go into the tens of thousands. I applied the learning and it's made all the difference in my life. The lessons helped form the pillars of my tremendous life.

And along the way I developed my very own tone of life. My hope has always been that others would see me as happy, cheerful, positive, encouraging, giving, loving, sharing, helping, understanding, forgiving, free from worry and fear, very content and very grateful.

I've always wanted others to see God at work through my life…that my life was one that was lived Inside Out…that I brought others joy and lifted them up and was always there for them.

How about your tone of life? How would the people in your personal and professional lives characterize it? Do they know what matters most to you? Is your tone of life what you want it to be?

No matter how you answered those questions, here's some tremendous advice on how to continuously improve your tone of life and how to enjoy a tremendous life…

Read to improve your life…seek counsel…be flexible…laugh at yourself…and live with gratitude.

That advice is from Charlie "Tremendous" Jones…the man who way back in 1963 patted a twelve year old boy on the head and told him that life is tremendous.

I was that boy. Charlie was right.

"Life is tremendous! It really is. You can be happy, involved, relevant, productive, healthy and secure in the midst of a high-pressure, commercialized, automated, pill-prone society. It's not easy nor automatic, but it's possible through the development of certain personal qualities which make up the traits of leadership.
Are you ready for leadership?
Whoo-hooo…let's go!"
Charles "Tremendous" Jones

Appendix A

SERVICE

To know WHAT to do is wisdom. To know HOW to do it is skill. To do the thing as it should be done is service. Most of us are wise and skillful...but it is service that prospers...SERVICE!

Brain service can be bought. Lip service can be hired. Physical service can be contracted for. But heart service is the kind you get when you pay with the coins of appreciation, kindness and consideration.

There is no influence in business as valuable as a kind voice...no stock in the store that equals in influence a friendly smile...no price has such small pulling power as dependable service...no advertising is so far reaching as the square deal.

SALESMANSHIP

Sell, satisfy, and make it pay and you'll live to sell another day.

Be careful to land the little fish, and by and by a big fish will bite...then all your experience with the little fish will come in handy.

Integrity, industry, common sense, sincerity, service and shoe leather...these are the useful tools in the kit for selling to satisfy.

Mix a little tolerance, some sympathy, and considerable cheerfulness with a lot of intelligent work. Then kindle the fire of kindness under this kettle and let the batch boil down. You can catch more customers with this syrup than you will catch with a vinegar face.

People study the art, or rather the achievement, of good salesmanship, but they often forget the one essential…the one factor that requires no schooling and this one factor comes without cost of money. Desire is the word…the desire to be honestly agreeable.

Study humans; anyone can sell bargains. Put yourself in the customer's place. Be fair and square with him and you will be fair and square with yourself. Make a friend of the customer.

If you want to have the spotlight on you, do something worthwhile and the spotlight will follow you. Do nothing worthwhile and the darkness will hide you.

The scheme of success is not to make yourself bigger than your job, but it is to make your job smaller than you. When you accomplish this, you will not have to go about looking for a bigger opportunity.

ADVERSITY

Prosperity deceives, adversity instructs.

Adversity is not the worst thing in life. Adversity is the turn in the road. It is not the end of the trail, unless you give up.

Adversity is often a forerunner of prosperity. One day in the school of adversity will teach a person more than a full term in the deceit of fortune.

MISTAKES

Clinging to past mistakes, as a fond memory, is like hanging a heavy anvil around your neck after you have fallen overboard.

My word to the man who feels he is making too many mistakes is this: Mistakes are absolutely necessary for personal progress, individual growth, and commercial conquest.

When you blunder, do not jump to the conclusion that the chapter of success in your life is closed. When you blunder, the world will give you credit for ambition, provided that you continue to try.

Man's mistakes are not due to his being a greenhorn, a novice, a dreamer or a lubber. Man's mistakes are largely due to his not thinking ahead.

BUSINESS

Business is never good business until it makes a friend.

Business is made up of the hands and hearts, thoughts and the heartthrobs of an organization. Merchandise is merely the sold stuff.

No matter how bad your business is, it is sure to be worse if you lose your courage.

SUCCESS

Success is not a chance shot...it is a slow, patient result of trying.

I know it is hard to work and to wait, but that is the only way to win…work and wait.

Every success has the cost marked in plain sight…w-o-r-k.

Keep both eyes open for the little things…the big things you can see with one eye closed.

Hidden in the soul of every man or woman…concealed in the heart of every human…is the statue of some success, be it great or small.

VOICE

Words are but tools…the voice conveys the meaning.

The tone of the voice tells whether you are friendly or are looking for a fight.

The average person is more susceptible to the change in tone in the voice than to any selected set of words.

The sound of the human voice betrays the speaker, for the sound comes from the soul, while words fly off the tongue.

The quality of a voice is singularly affecting. An insult in words can be so clothed that it affords no excuse for resentment. It is not so much what you say as how you say it.

YESTERDAY

Our mistakes of yesterday are not mistakes when they serve as guides for tomorrow. They are guides, not mistakes.

Yesterday was put there to help us keep today. "Do-it-today" is a good slogan, but here is a better one: "It was done yesterday."

TODAY

Today is for action, not talk.

Today's results are the only records that give advantage to the resources of business.

Today is all you have. Tomorrow is a promissory note, and yesterday is a cancelled check. Act today!

TOMORROW

We do not own one minute of tomorrow.

The person who constantly puts things off until tomorrow will continue to struggle with failure.

The day is lost that does not add to your stock of knowledge something that will help you tomorrow.

Every tomorrow is worth a lifetime of yesterday. Today we put the experience of yesterday to work to pay us rewards tomorrow.

The question "How's business today?" is the small and in-growing inventory. "How's business tomorrow?" is the big and building thought.

Appendix B

This is from a column Charlie wrote several years ago. It's called "A Sense Of Urgency". Within the column, Charlie shares his famous *7 Laws of Leadership*...

****

If you could add one personality trait to improve yourself, what would you choose? Courage? Wisdom? Enthusiasm? Confidence? We could go on and on and still probably miss the one you might choose.

I heard a speaker say it was important to be inspired but still more important to have the desire, the will to want to. I most heartily agree with him.

I also like Dr. Norman Vincent Peale's six-point success formula: 1. work, 2. work, 3. work, 4. forget self, 5. set goals, and 6. get along with others. We've all heard many, many formulas and they all will work if we will.

Most are ready to accept these success formulas but for some reason never get them into high gear. You've noticed many who have great potential and every reason to be tremendously successful, but nothing seems to happen.

What is it that chains so many of us to the pit of mediocrity? What is it that dampens the fires of greatness that are lit so many times in our hearts?

Perhaps my findings are not the only solution, but with all my heart I believe the fires of greatness in our hearts can be kept aglow only after we develop a sense of urgency and importance of what we are doing.

I mean a sense of urgency to the extent that we feel it is a matter of life and death; and it is a matter of life and death, for in growing we are alive and in quitting we are dying in a sense.

If you don't believe this, talk to anyone who has lost the sense of urgency of getting things done and has been drifting in complacency, mediocrity and failure. If you are without a sense of urgency in your work, you know what I mean.

A sense of urgency is that feeling that lets you know yesterday is gone forever, tomorrow never comes. Today is in your hands. It lets you know that shirking today's task will add to wasted yesterdays and postponing today's work will add to tomorrow's burden.

The sense of urgency causes you to accomplish what today sets before you. Thank God for the sense of urgency that can change a dull shabby job into a sparkling career. While this may not be the complete solution, I think we can all agree this will be a tremendous step in the right direction. Right now, ask God to give you a sense of urgency in your work. Believe that He did, and then act accordingly.

To help our sense of urgency help us, let's look at seven tremendous laws of leadership and follow that up with an examination of two important qualities—discipline and loyalty.

1. Learning to Put Excitement In Your Work

Why is it that some people work and work, and never have anything to show for it? And others do less and accomplish more? The secret is learning to put excitement in your work.

If I'm not learning to get excited about what I don't like, I'll never get much to be excited about what I do like.

Everybody looks for "the right job." Sometimes, you'll hear "I'm looking for a job that fits me." I say, "I hope you get something better than that." We need to be learning that no job can make you, but anyone that can put excitement into their work can make a job.

2. Use or Lose

There's a law that says we all have certain attributes, characteristics, and talents. If you use what you have, you'll get more; but if you don't use it, you'll lose it.

One night, as I was coming out of a seminar, a person asked, "do you think it's possible for someone to be excited about their business, be thrilled and successful, and then, three years later, be sick and sorry they ever heard of the whole business?" Here's a perfect example of one who doesn't know the law of *Use or Lose*.

Once he was in his glory, using all the talents he had. As a result, he was successful. But one morning, because he wasn't using what he had, he began losing it. And one morning he woke up and asked, "What went wrong? Who let me down?"

The answer is that nobody let him down. Nothing went wrong. Because he wasn't using what he had, he was losing it. And the people who lose it always blame somebody else. Remember, nobody is ever a failure until they blame someone else.

3. Give to Get

Leadership is learning to give whether or not you get anything in return. If you ever give to get something, you're not giving; you're trading. And there's a big difference between giving and trading.

If a person gives whether or not they get anything in return, then they are learning to give. If you give whether or not you get anything, you get a greater capacity to give more, whether or not you get anything in return.

And out of this begins to develop a reservoir of reserve and readiness that becomes a tremendous asset. You can lose your reputation, you can lose your home, you can even lose your family, but you can't lose your capacity to give once you've begun to live this law.

4. Production to Perfection

Someone will say, "I'm a perfectionist. I believe in doing everything perfectly, and if I can't do it perfectly, I won't do it." That's the person who never does anything.

There's a law that says if you're not learning to make something happen today you'll never know more than your own whimsical, shallow dreams. Production will teach you a little about perfection, but perfection will never be more than your own fantasy.

5. Exposure to Experience

In the beginning of life, God gives everybody an imaginary key ring. Every time a person exposes himself or herself to another situation they get another key of experience for their key ring. Soon, the key ring begins to fill with thousands and millions of keys of experience.

As a person gets exposure and experience, they get to use the same keys over and over again. The law of exposure to experience gets better with the years. Finally, a person gets to know which keys unlock which doors, while the inexperienced don't know if they have a key. All they can do is fumble around and hope to add another key of experience to their key ring.

6. Flexible Planning

This is the age of the planner. Everybody's planning, planning, planning. Don't ever tell anyone that planning will do it. I believe you have to have a plan to exist, but the real law is not planning; it's *Flexible Planning*.

Flexible planning says, "Plan on it going wrong." You say, "what if it goes right?" We will just have to work it in. Growing is learning that nothing ever goes wrong except to make you more right.

7. Motivated to Motivating

Which would you rather be: a miserable motivator or a happy motivated flop? I would rather be a happy, motivated flop, because if I can be motivated long enough, I'll get to be motivating, and if I can be motivated long enough, I'll eventually become a motivator.

And I'll get to enjoy what I get. That's not the case with the person who has learned to motivate everybody but themselves. Our problem isn't motivating them, but keeping them from demotivating me. The motivation will flow when you are totally committed and involved.

We live in a world where these two great words—discipline and loyalty—are becoming meaningless. Does this mean that they are worthless? On the contrary, they are becoming priceless qualities because they are so hard to develop in the first place.

And should you be one of the fortunate few who by God's grace have caught the vision, your battle has just begun because the greatest battle is to keep what you've learned through these two priceless qualities.

Discipline is that great quality that few people use that enables them to be constructively busy all the time. Even in discouragement and defeat, discipline will rescue you and usher you to a new place to keep constructively busy while you forget about doubt, worry and self-pity.

Oh, that more men and women in this day would realize the absolute necessity of discipline and the degree of growth and happiness to be attained from it.

Most people think that loyalty is to a thing or to a person when actually it is really to one's own self. Some think that it is to a goal or an objective, but again it is to one's own convictions.

If loyalty has to be earned then it is deserved and is hardly more than devoted emotion based on a temporary feeling.

No, loyalty is the character of a person who has given himself to the task before him and he will always realize that out of a loyal heart will spring all the other virtues that make life one of depth and growth.

Appendix C

Tremendous Jimmy's maxims were powerful,
sometimes funny, often profound.
Some belonged to well-known thinkers and writers.
Others he created during his distinguished career.
Here are his favorites, the ones he used with clients from his
private law practice and his bank trust department days...

****

Christopher Chapton died in 1680 and was buried in Westminster Abbey. His tombstone reads as follows:

> What I gave, I have.
> What I spent, I had.
> What I left, I lost.

Plan as though to live forever and live as though to die this day.

Happiness is choice.

Don't let yesterday use up too much of today.

The trouble with a man or woman who works like a horse is that all he or she wants to do evenings is hit the hay.

A person's worth is not measured by a balance sheet but rather by how he or she lives.

Some people seem to get the idea they're worth a lot of money just because they're rich.

Anyone who measures value by dollars is sure to be cheated.

Be sure to eat with the rich but go play with the poor who are more likely capable of joy.

General Eisenhower was right. He said you do not lead by hitting people over the head...that's assault, not leadership.

Setting an example is the only means of influencing another.

We have an economist at the bank. An economist is a person who can tell you what is going to happen next month then explain a month later why it didn't.

Will and Ariel Durant put it best: civilizations begin with faith and stoicism then end with skepticism and unbelief and an undisciplined pursuit of individual pleasure. A civilization is born stoic and dies epicurean.

A depression is a period when people do without the things their parents never had.

I saw an ad for a luxury condominium. It said, "now living well is the best investment". But the truth is that always living well is the only investment.

I find the older we are the more concerned we are about spending principal, yet each day we live is one less day we have to finance. Consider the maxim that says "It's better to live rich than die rich".

You may not know when you're well off but the Internal Revenue Service surely does.

Five Pillars of a Tremendous Life

There are two great agencies for redistribution of wealth: taxes and children.

You can't teach an old dogma new truths.

Thoreau was right; only that day dawns to which we are awake.

No deal is a good deal unless it's good for everyone involved.

As Einstein said, "the value of a person is what he or she gives, not what he or she is able to receive".

The pathway to truth is always open.

As Emerson said, "nothing great was ever achieved without enthusiasm".

As Freud put it, "being entirely honest with oneself is a good exercise".

It's important that people know what you stand for…and sometimes it's more important that they know what you won't stand for.

Appendix D

The following "Daily Dozen" constitutes the personal creed of Robert Louis Stevenson. He kept a piece of paper affixed to his bathroom wall with these twelve items on it in his own handwriting. As he'd shave every morning, he'd read the dozen.

****

1. Make up your mind to be happy. Learn to find pleasure in simple things.

2. Make the best of your circumstances. No one has everything, and everyone has something of sorrow intermingled with the gladness of life. The trick is to make the laughter.

3. Don't take yourself too seriously. Don't think that somehow you should be protected from misfortunes that befall others.

4. You can't please everybody. Don't let criticism worry you.

5. Don't let your neighbor set your standards. Be yourself.

6. Do the things you enjoy doing, but stay out of debt.

7. Don't borrow trouble. Imaginary things are harder to bear than the actual ones.

8. Since hate poisons the soul, do not cherish enmities,

grudges. Avoid people who make you unhappy.

9. Have many interests. If you can't travel, read about new places.

10. Don't hold postmortems. Don't spend your life brooding over sorrows and mistakes. Don't be one who never gets over things.

11. Do what you can for those less fortunate than yourself.

12. Keep busy at something. A very busy person never has time to be unhappy.

Appendix E

These "Paradoxical Commandments" were written by Kent Keith at the age of nineteen when he was a student at Harvard University. They represent Inside Out Living and Tone of Life at their very best. They're tremendous!

****

1. People are sometimes illogical, unreasonable, and self-centered.
    Love them anyway.

2. If you do good, people will sometimes accuse you of selfish, ulterior motives.
    Do good anyway.

3. If you are successful, you will win false friends and true enemies.
    Succeed anyway.

4. The good you do today might be forgotten tomorrow.
    Do good anyway.

5. Honesty and frankness make you vulnerable.
    Be honest and frank anyway.

6. The biggest men and women with the biggest ideas can be shot down by the smallest men and women with the smallest minds.
    Think big anyway.

7. People favor underdogs, but follow only top dogs.
   Fight for a few underdogs anyway.

8. What you spend years building may be destroyed overnight.
   Build anyway.

9. People really need help, but may attack you if you do help them.
   Help people anyway.

10. Give the world the best you have and you'll sometimes get kicked in the teeth.
    Give the world the best you have anyway.

Thank You...Thank You...Thank You!

To Tremendous Debbie
This book could not have been written without all the unwavering and faithful support and love and encouragement from you, my love. You're the best and I thank you so much!

To Tremendous Gloria Jones
On behalf of over 100 million people worldwide over the last five decades, allow me to thank you for sharing your tremendous husband with us! The sacrifices you made were many and they remain untold. But we all know that Charlie's success in life and business would have never happened without you and your support. Thank you Gloria...you're an unsung hero! God bless you!

To Tremendous Tracey and Tremendous Q
A special thank you to you two young, talented ladies for challenging me to write this book...the e-mails and phone calls to encourage me, shepherd the project, review numerous drafts, and suggest tweaks and edits. Whatever I did, you made it better!

To Tremendous Q and Dean
Thank you for the tremendous work on the documentary film about Charlie "Tremendous" Jones' life. It will have a life of it's own...and will be viewed by so many people in the years to come...just as Charlie envisioned it. Well done. You two are consummate professionals and I'm proud to say I know you!

To my Tremendous "read and review" Friends
No labor of love, as writing this book has been, comes to fruition without the help of friends...and I've had wonderful

friends volunteer to read drafts, help me fix mistakes, suggest an edit or two…or more, encourage me, and provide valuable feedback.

I'm indebted to Darryl McConnel, Jeanne Hardwick, Liz Clemm, Mike Loftus, Ian Larsen, Dwayne and Kate Alexander, Stephanie Jones, and Nadine Tereora. Thank you so much!

To YOU Tremendous Readers

Thank you for reading this book. I trust the book has been helpful to you. Here's to you living life Inside Out. And here's to your Tone of Life…may it always be as tremendous as you are!

About the Author

Charlie "Tremendous" Jones and author David Pierce

David Pierce is currently CEO of a major life insurance company in New Zealand.

Prior to coming to New Zealand, he lived in Hong Kong and was responsible for his company's marketing operations in Hong Kong, Macau, Singapore, Brunei, Malaysia, Thailand, Indonesia, and Vietnam.

He's a 30-year veteran of the life insurance and financial services industry, serving first as an Agent and Independent Financial Advisor, then in numerous sales management, senior management, marketing and leadership roles in the United States, Southeast Asia, India, and the South Pacific.

David holds a Bachelor of Arts from The American University, a Master of Arts from The University of Minnesota, and a Master of Science in Management from The American College. He also earned the Chartered Life Underwriter, Chartered Financial Consultant, and Chartered Leadership Fellow professional designations.

He served as Adjunct Professor of Business and Professional Communication at Western Kentucky University, and Adjunct Professor of Business and Economics at Middle Tennessee State University.

David is happily married, has two children, and four grandchildren.

Contact David Pierce to share your pillar experiences at:
www.FiveTremendousPillars.com
David@FiveTremendousPillars.com

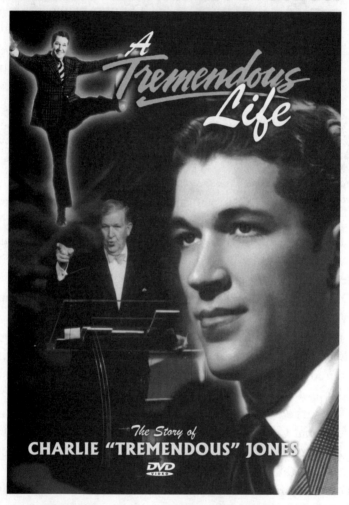